The
Parrot

An Owner's Guide To

A HAPPY HEALTHY PET

Howell Book House

Howell Book House
A Simon & Schuster Macmillan Company
1633 Broadway
New York, NY 10019

Library of Congress Cataloging-in-Publication Data
Freud, Arthur.
The parrot : an owner's guide to a happy, healthy pet / Arthur Freud.
p. cm.

ISBN 0-87605-497-1 (alk. paper)
1. Parrots. I. Title.
SF473.P3F736 1996   96-9031
636.6'865—dc20   CIP

Manufactured in the United States of America
10 9 8 7 6 5 4

Series Director: Dominique DeVito
Series Assistant Director: Ariel Cannon
Book Design: Michele Laseau
Cover Design: Iris Jeromnimon
Illustration: Ryan Oldfather
Photography:
   Front and back cover photos by Ron and Val Moat, inset: Pets by Paulette
   Joan Balzarini: 9, 13, 17, 18, 20, 21, 28, 35, 37, 40, 47, 48, 50, 52, 53, 57, 58, 63,
      64, 68, 69, 70, 71, 73, 76, 78, 79, 80, 81, 84, 85, 87, 97, 103, 104, 108, 111, 117
   Joan Blankenship: 7
   Paulette Braun/Pets by Paulette: 12, 14, 16, 19, 26, 38, 43, 44, 45, 46, 50, 60, 69, 72, 74,
      96, 98, 110, 112, 112, 116, 119
   Diane Clakins: 77
   Michael DeFraitas: 39, 49, 55, 60, 66–67
   Arthur Freud: 10, 39, 61, 89, 101
   Scott McKiernan/Zuma Press: 2–3, 5, 6, 41, 54, 74
   Ron and Val Moat: 30–31, 45, 56
   A.J. Mobbs: 88
   Positively Pets: 27
   Robert Pearcy: 25, 59, 62
   Pablo Tiengo: 36, 42, 51
   B. Everett Webb: 65, 115
   A. Wilson: 39
   Jean Wentworth: 11, 15, 22, 120–121
  Production Team: John Carroll, Kathleen Caulfield, Vic Peterson, Terri Sheehan,
   and Chris Van Camp

Contents

Welcome

to the

part one

World

of

the

Parrot

External Features of the Parrot

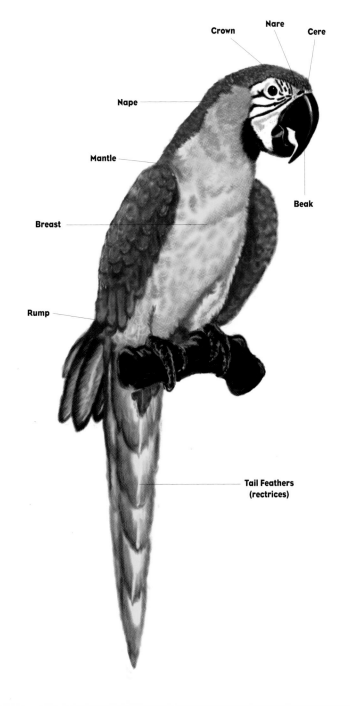

Crown

Nare

Cere

Nape

Mantle

Breast

Rump

Beak

Tail Feathers
(rectrices)

chapter 1

About

Parrots

The parrot family consists of more than 350 different species of birds. They include groups such as Amazons, African Greys, macaws, cockatoos, eclectus, conures, lories and lovebirds. Although most people do not realize it, technically even budgies and cockatiels are classified in the parrot family. Though they are small, they too possess the basic traits all parrots share, including a large, broad head, a short neck and a heavy, powerful beak with the upper beak overhanging the lower. Parrots' feet all have four toes, with two pointing forward and two backward.

Scarlet Macaw

5

Parrots are wild animals. Though they may be domestically bred and hand-fed, they have lived with human beings for two generations at most. How did parrots come to be one of the most popular pet birds, with over 1.2 million parrots in households around the United States?

The parrot family includes over 350 different species of birds, including the African Grey (on the left) and the Yellow-naped Amazon.

Parrots' ancestors developed 35 million years ago, the descendants of reptiles whose scales mutated into useful flying technology. Flying gave these new creatures a whole new niche to populate and thrive in; they had advantages in both finding food and fleeing predators and the new creatures flourished and continued to evolve and adapt. Parrot fossils millions of years old have been found in England, France, Australia, Africa and South America.

History of Parrot Keeping

Parrots have adapted to life in jungle environment over millions of years. However, human beings have long had a fascination with these beautiful creatures and have kept them as pets for centuries.

PARROTS IN CLASSICAL CIVILIZATION

According to some sources, parrots were introduced to Greco-Roman civilization after Alexander the Great returned from his Indian expedition. These first imported parrots were probably Ringnecks from India or related islands. In Greek and Roman culture, these exotic birds were housed in beautiful cages of precious materials, and were worth a great deal of money.

PARROTS IN EUROPE

After Vasco de Gama found a sea route to Europe, parrot importation increased. The birds no longer had to be funneled through third parties in Arab countries. This elimination of the third party made parrot prices slightly more reasonable, and these birds became more widely available and popular. Keep in mind, however, that parrot availability was still limited to the highest echelons of society. Keeping an ornamental animal that did no useful work around the farm or home was entirely out of reach for the average citizen.

In the last twenty years, parrots have become one of the most popular pet birds in America. (Yellow-fronted Amazon)

Typically, many members of European royal families had parrots. Henry VIII had an African Grey with manners allegedly as bad as his own. And Columbus purportedly brought back a pair of Cuban Amazons to Queen Isabella when he returned from his first expedition to the Americas.

Global exploration increased during the eighteenth century and flourished especially during the nineteenth century. Ventures to the New World to learn about the creatures, geography and exploitable resources of the continent were common. Knowledge about parrots increased with every venture intended to understand, observe or even capture them. Victorians made great strides and showed great interest in understanding the physical and behavioral mechanisms of these new creatures. Though their methods may be considered unethical by today's standards, their research and understanding contributed immeasurably to many sciences, including the modern study of biology, natural history and the environment.

In addition to studying parrots at great length, the Victorians were also the first to truly popularize these birds. The Victorian sensibility was intrigued by these exotic creatures who mimicked the sounds of human voices. A parlor in a well-done home was incomplete without a parrot. Parrot popularity reached an all-time high during the end of the last century.

In the 1920s, however, several outbreaks of parrot-related diseases frightened prospective owners and the public at large. In the United States, a ban on parrot importation was enacted in 1946, though lifted in 1967. Throughout the next decades, outbreaks of parrot-related diseases, often caused by inadequate quarantine periods, caused the government to implement several restrictions on parrot importation. However, new quarantine procedures and an immense increase in the numbers of birds who are bred in captivity has allowed parrots to once again be kept without fear of contagious disease.

PARROT TRAITS

Though parrots vary greatly in almost every respect, the characteristics found in all parrot species serve to classify them together. These traits include:

- Large head

- Short neck

- Four toes, two pointing forward and two backward

- Large beak, with upper overhanging lower

The Parrot in the United States

Parrot Importation

The popularity of these birds in this country has fluctuated with changes in prices, lifestyles and availability. Before the 1970s, parrots were imported, then banned when outbreaks of parrot-related diseases arose. These bans didn't stop illegal imports from entering the country, but in 1973 quarantine stations were established in the United States, allowing birds to be safely imported. A period of vast importation of parrots followed, lasting almost twenty years. By the end of this period many countries had imposed restrictions on exporting their exotic wildlife. In 1992, the Wild Bird Conservation Act became law in the United States and effectively ended all importation of parrots.

The domestically bred parrots available today are healthier than their imported ancestors and have bonded with humans since birth.

There was only a limited amount of domestic breeding of parrots until the mid 1980s. Most of the parrots purchased during the 1970s and early 1980s were imports and required a quarantine period and a considerable amount of taming and training when they were finally brought home. These birds were not always easy to work with as they had experienced a certain degree of trauma in being captured, exported and then moved from quarantine to distributor to pet shop to final owner. In addition, the thirty-day quarantine period involved medication with heavy doses of chlortetracycline. This regimen prevented the release of any parrots carrying an infectious disease. Unfortunately, thirty days of such strong medication can have a negative effect on a parrot's spleen and liver.

Today, domestically bred offspring of imported parrots, like these two baby African Greys, are available.

PARROT CONSERVATION

For many reasons, including habitat destruction and excessive capture of parrots for the wildlife trade, many populations of parrots are now threatened in their native habitats. Many measures have been enacted to stop the endangerment of these beautiful birds. The continued importation of parrots into the United States has been effectively halted by the Wild Bird Importation Act of 1992. International treaties, namely the Convention on International Trade in Endangered Species of Flora and Fauna (CITES), also limit the importation of wildlife. In many cases, captive breeding may be the only way to keep up population levels, and there are many species of endangered parrots which you should never consider keeping if you do not plan to breed them. Become involved in the parrot conservation effort by learning about these magnificent birds in their natural homes and in

**FAMOUS
OWNERS OF
PARROTS**

Robin Williams

Elizabeth Taylor

King George V

Theodore
Roosevelt, Jr.

Paul Bowles

Andrew
Jackson

captivity. Educate yourself on the conditions of their habitats and species preservation, and help make others aware of these conditions. See Chapter 9, "Resources," for the names and addresses of parrot conservation groups.

DOMESTICALLY BRED PARROTS

The parrots available today are all domestically bred birds. In most cases they have been hand-fed by their breeder, or their hand-feeding has been completed in the pet shop in which they are for sale. These birds are tamer and healthier than imported parrots. When purchased at an early age, the new owner has an opportunity to bond with the bird from

In the 1970s and 1980s, parrots were imported to the United States from their jungle homes in South America, Australia and southern Asia.

the time it is weaned. Some people even choose to take a baby parrot home before it is fully weaned and complete the hand-feeding themselves. This enables them to establish an excellent relationship with the new pet as the baby parrot assumes that the person feeding it is its parent.

The Parrot as a Pet

For many people the term *pet* usually brings to mind a dog or cat. The more adventurous among us may consider as pets other furry beasts such as rabbits, guinea pigs, chinchillas or even ferrets. Why have so many hundreds of thousands of people chosen parrots as their preferred companions over the last twenty-five years?

Many pet lovers become involved with parrots because of the birds' unusual personalities. Parrots are feisty, independent and highly intelligent creatures who will accept and return large amounts of affection when they wish to share their time with you. The operative phrase here is "when they wish," as trying to force a parrot to play or roughhouse when he isn't interested is asking to be rebuffed. People who love parrots value this strong personality and unique behavior because they are indicative of the intelligence of these birds. In spite of parrots' strong personalities, you will find that once your bird has learned to trust you he will exhibit a strong desire to please you because for much of the day, he actually wants your company.

People are attracted to parrots because of their entertaining antics and beautiful coloring. (Scarlet Macaws)

PARROT PERSONALITY

Your parrot will demonstrate feelings of affection and attachment by saying and doing the things he knows attract your attention. Parrots twist their bodies and swing upside down when favored people are in their room. Many parrots who just utter a few words when you are watching them will go through an entire repertoire when you start to leave. After years of observing parrot behavior, I am convinced they are fully aware that a large part of their comfort and happiness depends on their owner's good will. If you give a parrot the opportunity to be friendly and charming, he will take it and become an important part of your family and your life.

Not every parrot welcomes petting or cuddling, although some show inordinate pleasure in such activities and thrive on close physical contact with their owners. The wise owner will learn to be aware of certain subtle hints the parrot provides to indicate that he does not want to be scratched or even touched. He may be tired or hungry or just plain unwilling to have you pick him up. If you attempt to force yourself on him, it is to be expected that he will resist either by retreating from you or by biting if provoked.

Many parrots, like this cockatoo, enjoy closeness and physical contact with their owners.

Some parrots develop the reputation of being "one-person birds," but this attitude is based mostly on who feeds them and cleans their cage. A great deal of subtle interaction goes on between the parrot and the person who completes these tasks on a regular basis.

Parrots are fascinating to people because they exhibit a high level of curiosity about their surroundings

13

and the objects and toys in their environment. A dog may sniff at a ball or toy bone, but a parrot will examine a new toy from every angle before getting close to it. If he considers it threatening, he may avoid it until he decides it's safe. Once he is sure about the item, he will play with it and may even devise ingenious games you and the toy manufacturer never contemplated.

The Double-yellow Head's comical personality and lively behavior make it a favorite pet.

Famous Parrots

Parrots have become very popular for use in advertising. In print media, they are frequently used to summon up exotic locales, although occasionally the ad director will get it all wrong and show a cockatoo showing off in a South American palm tree. In spite of errors like this, parrot lovers are always thrilled when they see their pets publicized.

Many celebrities keep parrots and have done so for a long time. King George V owned a white cockatoo. Robin Williams has a Double-yellow Head and Elizabeth Taylor has been photographed in her swimming pool with a pair of Yellow-naped Amazons.

Parrots exhibit a high degree of curiosity about objects in their environment.

At one time only royalty or the very rich could own these exotic creatures, but today parrots are available to all of us.

chapter 2

Selecting
the Right
Parrot

Blue and Gold Macaws

When you finally get down to making the actual choice and purchase of your new pet, you must consider several issues. The parrot you finally decide to purchase should be one who fits in well with your family and living arrangements. Choose the right parrot from the beginning, and you will not have to deal with the tragedy of having to give your parrot up because it does not suit your lifestyle or your neighbors.

Noise Considerations

Parrots communicate through whistles and screams, which can be quite loud. Many parrots will announce their presence by saying or shouting the words and phrases they have learned in your home. To most parrot owners, this is a lovely noise. If, however, you are in tight quarters and the noise of a loud parrot will disturb friends and neighbors, select your parrot from those considered to be the least noisy, like parakeets, lories or conures.

Cockatoos are among the loudest of the parrots. Their size permits a large volume of air to be expelled from their lungs and this enables them to produce a loud scream. Like most parrots, cockatoos will usually squawk in the morning when they greet the day. They will also scream if you are late with evening repasts and attention. Some cockatoos, such as the Moluccans, produce a loud hooting call as part of their display behavior and frequently accompany it by stamping one foot up and down. This is charming unless your neighbor is also stamping his foot or pounding on your wall.

Cockatoos are large, intelligent birds, but their tendency to make lots of noise doesn't make them perfect for apartment living.

Macaws are almost as loud as the cockatoos but their screams are higher pitched and thus may be even more disturbing. Typically, macaws engage in morning and evening "jungle calls," which are fine for Tarzan movies but may prove a problem if those living close to you do not appreciate them.

The Amazon family is less noisy but this is a comparative description. Amazons will engage in loud whistles and screams many times during the day and evening, but their volume should normally not be a problem to immediate neighbors. Size is also a factor here; you will find the large Mealy Amazon, Double-yellow Heads and Yellow-naped Amazons make more noise than the Green-cheeked or Yellow-fronted Amazon. Unfortunately the former are much better talkers, and if you choose on noise volume alone you may be rejecting the most interesting of the Amazons.

African Greys are a good choice for those who cannot tolerate consistently loud noises. The African Grey tends to whistle more than scream and usually speaks at a moderate volume. These little chatterboxes also enjoy making a knocking sound that appears to be done with their beak and voicebox, and can be loud and start-

The Double-yellow Head Amazon will delight you with his speech capacity, but he may also disturb neighbors with his loud screams.

ling. His whistles can be piercing but, as mentioned above, this is a form of communication and so does not happen continually. When I would move one of two Greys out of my bird room to let it socialize with family members in the living room, the African Grey who had been left behind would produce a chorus of these whistles and the upstairs bird would reply to him.

Lories and lorikeets, conures, eclectus, lovebirds and long-tailed parakeets such as the Ringnecks are all fairly quiet birds. The same is also true of cockatiels and budgies. You may find that the cries they do make are fairly high-pitched and some people find this objectionable.

The descriptions I have given you are "worst case" and you should spend some time with the parrot you are interested in to see if you can survive even if he does have the ability to scream. Parrots do not engage in this behavior constantly, and for some people the sounds eventually become part of the background noise in their households.

Spatial Considerations

While you are thinking about how much noise you and
your neighbors can tolerate, it is a good idea to think
about how much space you have in your home to keep
a bird. Cage size will be determined by the size of the
bird. In most (but not all) cases the larger the cage the
better. The exceptions are very small or very young
birds who may find it difficult to maneuver in a large
cage. Do you have room for the large cage a macaw or
cockatoo will need? Will a cage this large crowd the
room to an uncomfortable degree? Before you choose
a parrot, make sure you have
enough space for you both to be
comfortable. (See chapter 4 on
housing for recommended cage
sizes.)

A macaw will need lots of space in
a cage—and out of the cage.
They are large birds with powerful beaks. Their strength can be
used for play but it can also be
turned to destructive behavior.
Your macaw will need a place
where he can have a bit of free-
dom without chewing the legs off valuable furniture. If
you don't have this kind of space, you may want to
ignore the bird's bright colors and get a smaller parrot.

*A macaw's
large and pow-
erful beak can
prove destruc-
tive to your fur-
niture, so make
sure you have
"parrot-proof"
space for this
large bird to
exercise in.*

Lories and lorikeets aren't large birds and don't
require huge cages. However, they do require a diet
heavy in liquid, and their droppings reflect this.
Although recent nutritional advances have made some
dietary modifications possible, birds in this group are
difficult to keep in an apartment.

Shedding

Cockatoos are unique among parrots in that they constantly shed small particles of feathers in the form
of feather dust. This keeps their feathers clean and
attractive but may be a problem to a family where one
or more members are sensitive to these particles.

Consider having the whole family visit the bird you are going to buy and stay with him long enough to see if anyone has an adverse reaction.

Parrots with Children

The presence of children in your home is a factor that should be considered when making your choice about

a parrot. Children who are able to reason will understand the danger of putting their fingers through the bars of a cockatoo's or macaw's cage. You can explain to intelligent youngsters that these birds can exert great pressure with their beaks and do considerable damage to a finger placed through the bars of a cage. (Most parrots see such indignities as a great challenge and will bite to get that finger out of their space.) Young children may tell you they understand but they and their friends may still be tempted to take a chance. Unless you have a way of keeping the birds in a secure room when you are not present I would think carefully about buying a cockatoo or macaw if you have very young children at home.

African Greys are smaller than macaws and cockatoos, and may be more suitable as a family pet.

Amazons, African Greys, eclectus, conures and lovebirds can give sharp nips but do not pose an actual danger to little fingers. My African Greys seem to favor a special "cuticle bite" which is painful enough to make anyone think twice about putting their fingers in the Grey's cage, but not hard enough to be truly dangerous.

Ringnecks and others in their family as well as caiques, lories and lorikeets, cockatiels and budgies do not pose a real biting problem. Of course, if you take normal precautions and have young children who can understand the dangers of large beaked birds, you may be able to buy the parrot you want rather than selecting one of the "safe" birds.

Parrots and Other Pets

The presence of other pets in your home is another factor to consider when you are making your purchase. If you have other parrots, you may be used to letting them out to move freely about the room in which their cage is located.

When you introduce two parrots, especially large ones like the cockatoo and Amazon above, supervise the situation until you are sure the birds are friendly.

If your bird is smaller and tries to climb on the cage of a newly arrived macaw, cockatoo or Amazon, it may lose a toe or worse. Do not plan to house large and small birds together. In general, all parrots (except for those you are trying to breed) should be kept in separate cages.

PARROTS WITH DOGS AND CATS

Cats are natural hunters and may be attracted to the quick movements of a smaller parrot. Larger birds, such as cockatoos and macaws, generally fare better with cats, though their large size and strength don't guarantee any protection from an unfriendly dog.

But it is possible for your parrot to become friends with the dog or cat in your household. Supervise their interactions at all times when your parrot is out of the cage, and use common sense. A dog who chases anything that moves is probably not a candidate for a parrot pal.

Price and Availability

Before setting your heart on a particular species be sure that the bird you are seeking is actually available.

Searching for rare or totally unavailable birds is frustrating and disappointing.

You also need to make sure the parrot you want is in your price range. The prices listed below will vary with supply and demand and the time of the year. If you are willing to consider an older "baby" parrot you might want to do your shopping in September or October. At that time, most babies from the spring and summer clutches will have been sold and the breeder or pet shop owner may feel pressured to sell his remaining parrots at a lower price to move them out before new babies, who will appear much cuter, arrive.

Large parrots, especially, can be friends with dogs and cats, but make sure their interactions are well supervised.

AMAZONS

In the Amazon family you should be able to find Yellow-naped, Double-yellow Head, Blue-fronted, Green-cheeked, Mealy, Spectacled, Red-lored, Lilac-crowned and Orange-winged Amazons. The parents of these parrots were all imported in great numbers during the 1970s and early 1980s, and many aviculturists are breeding them and selling hand-fed chicks. Finding a Tres Marias subspecies of the Double-yellow Head or the highly verbal Panama Amazon is a much greater challenge. Some of the most beautiful and desirable Amazons, such as the St. Vincent or Cuban, are on the endangered species list. Thus, they are not only very rare but trade in them is restricted.

Prices for hand-fed baby versions of the Amazons listed above will range from approximately $700 to about $1,500. Yellow-napes and Double-yellow Heads will be at the high end while the Spectacled and Orange-winged Amazons will command lower prices.

AFRICAN GREYS

African Greys are readily available. The typical price for a hand-fed chick is about $1,200. A subspecies, the Timneh Grey, can cost as little as $750.

MACAWS

Among the full-sized macaws you will find Blue and Gold and Scarlet Macaw chicks easiest to locate. Large numbers of them were previously imported and many of these birds have been paired and are now in breeding setups. In addition, Blue and Gold and Scarlet Macaws are easier to breed in captivity than many other macaws.

It may seem incongruous but the expensive and highly desired Hyacinth Macaw is also being regularly bred, and chicks are often available. These big birds require very large flights for breeding and even individual birds need cages that will dominate a room. Breeders charge upwards of $8,000 for a hand-fed chick and have no trouble getting that price.

> **THINGS TO LOOK FOR WHEN CHOOSING YOUR PARROT**
>
> Sleek feathers
>
> Firm droppings
>
> Curious, energetic behavior

Green-winged Macaws and Military Macaws are less common and less popular. Prices for these parrots are about $1,700. You will also occasionally find hybrid macaws offered for sale. The best known macaw hybrids are Blue and Gold/Scarlets called Catalinas, Scarlet/Green-wings known as Rubies, Scarlet/Militaries called Shamrocks and Blue and Gold/Green-wings, which are referred to as Harlequins. Most aviculturists and breeders frown upon hybridizing the large parrots as it dilutes the bloodlines of breeding stock.

Several smaller macaws, usually grouped as the "mini-macaws," are also available. These include the Yellow-collared or Yellow-naped Macaw, Severe and Hahns Macaws. The Yellow-naped is the largest and most talkative of the three and because of extensive domestic breeding it is also generally the most easy to locate. Prices for the Yellow-collared and the Severe are about $800; the Hahns commands a lower price of about $600.

COCKATOOS

Chicks from Moluccan, Umbrella, Goffin's, Rose-breasted and subspecies of the Sulfur-crested Cockatoo are often found at breeders and in pet shops. Moluccans sell for about $1,400 to $1,800. Birds who are a deep pink bring the higher prices. Umbrellas can be found for $1,000 to $1,400. Rose-breasteds will generally cost anywhere from $1,200 to $1,500.

When considering Sulfur-crested chicks you may be offered a "true *Galerita galerita*" chick as opposed to what is referred to as a Triton. The terms refer to the parenthood of the birds; *Galerita galerita* descends from Australian birds and Tritons are the offspring of cockatoos originally imported from Indonesia. The differences will be noted in chapter 3, but unless you have a specific reason to want the Australian version, either one makes a delightful pet. You can assume that *Galerita galerita* will cost at least $2,000 for a hand-fed baby while a Triton will have a lower price of about $1,500.

Yellow and Red-tailed Black Cockatoos, Palm Cockatoos and the exotically named Gang-gang Cockatoo are beautiful and interesting but it is doubtful that you will be able to obtain any of them. They are rare and endangered and most people never even get to see them outside of a zoo environment.

ECLECTUS

Members of the eclectus group are greatly admired for their beautiful coloring and glossy feathers. With the exception of several rare subspecies, you should have no trouble in finding these birds either at a pet shop or in the aviary of a breeder. The Solomon Island subspecies is often described as the best pet material among the eclectus but most fanciers find that all eclectus make good pets. Males generally sell for about $1,000, and females, who have more varied and brighter colors, for about $1,200. Although the colors of the female are more pleasing, don't reject a friendly male; both males and females make equally good pets.

RINGNECKS

Long-tailed parakeets such as the Ringnecks as well as conures, caiques and lovebirds are all regularly available for about $200 to $400 each. There are some rare mutations in the Ringneck family that cost much more but I would recommend the common, garden variety Ringnecks for those just starting out.

Where to Buy Your Parrot

When you are ready to buy a parrot you have several choices of where to make this important purchase. The most obvious would be a local pet shop. You can also try to find a local breeder or you can examine ads in one of the bird magazines and buy from a breeder who will ship the bird to you. You can even check the ads in your local newspaper, where you can almost always find birds listed for "adoption." Each of these methods has both advantages and disadvantages.

Lilac-crowned Amazons were imported into the United States during the 1970s and 1980s. Domestically bred descendants of those birds are available today.

25

PET SHOP BIRDS

Making your purchase from a local pet shop usually means that you are going to pay top dollar for your parrot. This is because in most cases the shop had to pay a breeder for the bird and then care for it and possibly finish its hand-feeding. In addition, pet shops, like all businesses, have overhead, and the price of anything they sell will include a portion of that overhead. If they didn't do this, they couldn't stay in business.

Today, the gorgeous Hyacinth Macaw is readily available, though quite expensive.

Buying from a local shop offers a number of advantages. Because it's local you can see the bird before you buy it. I recommend a number of visits over a period of days so you can get a good idea of the bird's temperament and vitality. I would hesitate to purchase a bird if each time that you observed it you found it was sitting quietly in a corner with its beak stuck in its shoulder feathers.

You should also **check for simple signs of poor health.** The most obvious things to look for would be loose droppings, evidence of current or past nasal discharge, lethargy and plucked feathers. A healthy and vigorous parrot will exhibit sleek feathers, firm droppings and will move about its cage and possibly perform some acrobatics while exhibiting a degree of curiosity about you.

A local purchase also permits you to **interact with the parrot before you buy it.** If it is out on a perch you can (with the shopkeeper's permission) attempt to make some sort of physical contact. This can take the form of touching its feet or even its beak or head. Be sure to move slowly and be prepared to retreat if the parrot attempts to bite. If, however, the parrot accepts these touches or, better still, seems to want more affection, you should definitely consider him for purchase. Beware of the shopkeeper who tells you that Godzilla the Yellow-nape is really a wonderfully tame bird and not to be put off by his savage attack. With parrots, what you see is what you get. If he attempts to bite you in the store he will do the same in your home.

When buying a baby bird from a pet shop **do not assume that just because it is a baby that it has been hand-fed.** Pet shops generally buy their birds from breeders. Many breeders do hand-feed their chicks and this almost always results in a wonderfully tame, people-loving bird. Sometimes, however, a breeder is overwhelmed with chicks or other activities and he decides to let the parent birds do the feeding of the young birds. These parrots will unfortunately not be much tamer than an imported wild bird. Of course, if there is a sizable price differential you can consider this type of young bird and plan to work at taming it yourself.

Some pet shops will offer you a baby bird they are hand-feeding but is not yet weaned. The owner may offer a discount of several hundred dollars if you are willing to finish the hand-feeding yourself. I do not recommend this unless you have had a good deal of prior experience in hand-feeding other birds such as cockatiels or budgies. If you are a novice at hand-feeding, errors in food temperature, consistency or even the diet itself may result in an impacted crop or the chick failing to eat. Birds have a very high metabolism, and failure to eat can become a serious problem in a very short time.

When you are choosing a bird, check for signs of good health, like sleek feathers, and a curious, energetic attitude.

A reputable pet shop will offer a guarantee on the bird you buy. Generally it is limited to a short period of time such as a week or less. Your receipt should state the species of the bird, that it is domestically bred (with it's band number listed on the receipt), that the bird is healthy and that you have the option of bringing it to a veterinarian for checking. If the vet testing indicates health problems you should then be permitted to return the bird for a refund. Be sure to get this guarantee in writing and make sure your guarantee notes the price that you paid and indicates "refund" rather than replacement, as you may have to wait quite a while for the pet shop to get a replacement of the type of parrot you want. If you are pleased with the shop you can always use the refund to buy the replacement bird from them.

You can get your baby bird directly from a breeder or though a pet shop. In either case, determine if the baby has been hand-fed or not. (Black-headed Caiques)

BUYING FROM A BREEDER

If you decide to purchase directly from a breeder you will be able to pay a much lower price than that asked in a pet shop. If the breeder is local, follow the same procedure regarding health and tameness that you would in a pet shop. Ask for a similar guarantee, but keep in mind that a breeder is in all likelihood operating out of his home, and may not stand behind the guarantee with the same support you can expect from a formal business.

Some breeders will not permit you in their aviaries. They may explain that this is a health precaution or that they want to avoid disturbing breeding pairs. It should be possible for you to peek into the aviary without actually entering, and I would insist on being permitted to do this before making a purchase. You may be dealing with "breeders" who do not have any adult birds and who are actually jobbers. Such individuals buy birds from true breeders and resell them at a profit. Some may not even have the baby birds available until they get your money, which they will then use to pay for the chick you have ordered. Dealing with such individuals offers no advantages to you.

Whether you buy your parrot from a pet store or a breeder, there are certain services you may wish to consider asking for. Even though the baby parrot has been guaranteed and presumably checked by a veterinarian, ask about having blood work and culturing done before you make your final payment and bring the baby home. The cost of this may run as high as $80 to $100 but it is a worthwhile investment in peace of mind to know that the health of your bird is perfect.

MICROCHIPPING AND SEXING

You may also wish to have the bird "microchipped" and sexed by the vet. Microchipping involves placing a minute computer-type chip under the skin of the bird. If, because of theft or other catastrophe, you ever need to make a positive identification of the bird, the microchip can be "read" by a scanning device and the information will prove that it is your bird.

Most pet parrots do not exhibit external sex characteristics. The males and females look the same in terms of size, coloring and behaviors. Exceptions are groups like the eclectus, in which males and females look very different. For other birds, sex must be determined through lab tests.

The current favored method of sexing is through the use of a high-powered microscope to view the chromosomes in the blood from a living feather. This method is painless, safe and accurate. Sexing should cost about $50 and microchipping about $25. If everything (including the blood tests and culturing) is done at one time it may cost less. You can also ask the seller of the bird to absorb some of the cost of these extras.

part two

Parrot Profiles

chapter 3

Parrot
Profiles

Solomon Island and Vosmaeri Eclectus

Parrot popularity is based on the nature of certain groups of birds in terms of their ability to become tame and trusting as well as that elusive trait that has always been associated with the parrot family—speech capacity. The status of parrots is also directly based on their availability. Although fantastic reputations can develop, no bird can actually be popular if people cannot buy it. When choosing your parrot, keep in mind that while the ability to speak is certainly a wonderful trait, charming and lovable behavior is just as important, perhaps even more so.

You will be attracted to many birds when you begin your search for a parrot. Keep the following information and your particular lifestyle limitations in mind when you make your purchase. Larger parrots will generally require more care and time and this should also be a factor in your choice. No one should buy a parrot if they cannot give it the care and attention it requires. These beautiful birds are not trophies or status symbols but highly intelligent living creatures who, if treated well, will reward your attention with a lifetime of loyalty and affection.

Amazon Parrots

The most popular members of this group are the Yellow-napes, Double-yellow Heads, Yellow-fronted, Blue-fronts, Mexican Red-heads and Mealy Amazons. Domestically raised chicks from all of these groups are now available on a regular basis. Many were imported during the 1970s and 1980s, and pairs from these imports are now producing on a fairly regular basis. People are attracted to Amazons because of their talking ability, attractive colors and playful nature. Provide an Amazon with the simplest toy, such as a block of wood or a bell, and his playful antics will amuse both you and him for many hours.

Amazons' eyes will dilate and contract rapidly when they are excited, frightened or extremely pleased. At the same time, they will fan out their tail feathers and ruffle the feathers of their neck in an effort to look intimidating. Don't be put off by this behavior; it does not mean that you are dealing with a savage beast—just one who is trying to bluff you into thinking he's larger and more dangerous than he really is.

THE YELLOW-NAPED AMAZON

The Yellow-naped Amazons are unique in terms of their capacity for speech. They all learn to speak and seem to do so without any extra tutelage on the part of their owners. I remember the owner of a Yellow-nape calling me to see if I wanted to purchase her parrot. She had a problem because the loquacious bird talked so much and so loudly that her husband said that it was either him or the bird! Not every Yellow-nape is this talented, but if you really worked at teaching a Yellow-nape clever expressions, you would probably wind up with a bird who'd get invited to perform on late-night talk shows.

Yellow-naped Amazon

The Yellow-nape is a fairly large Amazon that reaches lengths of about fourteen inches. It has the typical Amazon coloration of a green body with a lighter green on the lower surface. The beak is large and black except toward the base of the upper beak, where the color lightens to horn. The coarse, bristly feathers around the nostrils help to identify this parrot as does the yellow marking that appears on the rear crown and extends down the nape as the bird ages. The nape markings appear at about seven or eight months of age and in-crease in size until maximum development at about eighteen months.

Do not be confused if you are offered a Yellow-nape with a yellow marking on its forehead as well as the beginning of a nape marking. The subspecies of Yellow-napes from Honduras have this marking in addition to their yellow nape. Since the nape marking appears at a later age, young Yellow-napes from Honduras could be mistaken for Yellow-fronted Amazons if you are not familiar with their other characteristics.

Yellow-naped Amazons are charming and intelli-gent parrots, but many seem to develop a personality fault after they have matured. At about three or four years of age they become intensely possessive of the person who feeds and cares for them. This is manifested in biting if that person happens to be holding them and starts to pay attention to another bird or even to another human. This behavior may also be linked to the time of the year—it seems to be worst just before and during the breeding season. If you are going to keep a single parrot and you remember to give the bird your full attention while he's out of the cage, this type of behavior may not be a problem.

THE DOUBLE-YELLOW HEAD

The Double-yellow Head has been known as a pet for many years. Its breeding grounds in Mexico made it an obvious favorite in the southwestern United States and,

Double-yellow Head Amazon

prior to import regulations, it was common practice for visitors to Mexico to bring home a Double-yellow as a pet. During the period of great importation (1973–1985), vast numbers of these parrots entered the United States to become pets or breeders. Their domestically bred offspring are now often offered as prime pets by breeders and pet shops.

The Double-yellow Head is shorter than the Yellow-nape and is a stockier and more solidly built bird. Its name stems from the ability of this parrot to ruffle up its head and neck feathers to an amazing degree when it is excited or agitated, thus the fanciful designation of "double" yellow head. As with all the Amazons, its basic color is green, though it has red markings at the bend of the wings and a bright yellow head marking that develops from specks of yellow in young chicks to a complete yellow head and neck covering in older birds. A rare subspecies, the Tres Marias Amazon, has the yellow marking extending all the way down its back. The Double-yellow Head also has a band of yellow feathers above its feet that look like yellow booties. These markings, along with a white ring around the eye, give the bird a rather clownlike appearance, and the Double-yellow Head's behavior does nothing to discourage this impression. They swing upside down and scream endearments designed to attract visitors.

Double-yellow Heads are not as proficient at speech as Yellow-napes, but they are excellent mimics and singers. Many people prefer them because of their mild personalities and comical behavior.

THE YELLOW-FRONTED AMAZON

The Yellow-fronted Amazon is a close relative of the Double-yellow Head. It is a very popular and commonly kept parrot with a relatively small yellow marking on the top of the head. It is a fairly small Amazon but a very popular one. Its extensive range throughout Central and South America meant large numbers were available. Today, these birds are commonly bred and sold and can be found at lower prices than either the Double-yellow Head or the Yellow-nape. They are not as proficient at speaking

Yellow-fronted Amazon

but they can develop a small vocabulary and learn to mimic household sounds.

THE BLUE-FRONTED AMAZON

The Blue-fronted Amazon is sleek and handsome with a pale blue marking above the beak and between the eyes. There is considerable variation to the extent of this marking and it sometimes extends further back onto the crown. The Blue-front has a long history as a pet parrot, but its speech ability is often exaggerated. I would rate it as mediocre at best. You may find some shops offering a larger version of the Blue-front and referring to it as "Chaco" Blue-front. These parrots come from a different area of South America, and their size is the only thing that differentiates them from the standard Blue-front. The Blue-fronts I have owned were very clever and playful birds whose interesting behavior compensated for their marginal speaking talents.

Blue-fronted Amazon

THE ORANGE-WINGED AMAZON

The Orange-winged Amazon is often confused with the Blue-front, because it actually has a larger blue marking on its head than the Blue-front does. It has bright yellow cheeks and a patch of orange feathers on its wings. If in doubt about whether a bird is a Blue-front or an Orange-wing, check the beak color. The beak of the Blue-front is completely black while the Orange-wing has a horn-colored beak that becomes much darker at the tip.

Orange-winged Amazon

Huge numbers of Orange-winged Amazons were imported from South and Central America, and this volume and constant availability kept their prices at moderate levels. Although they are not highly rated talkers, tame, domestic chicks make good pets and can be considered excellent "starter" parrots.

THE GREEN-CHEEKED, OR MEXICAN RED-HEAD, AMAZON

The Green-cheeked Amazon or Mexican Red-head is another popular parrot that can be purchased at a moderate price. These small, thirteen-inch-long green birds have a vivid red crown and bright green cheeks. Their original popularity was established by their ori-

gin in northern Mexico, which, prior to restrictive legislation, made them perfect to bring home from a vacation. Great numbers were also legally imported during the 1970s and 1980s and, although they are not wonderful conversationalists, they are active birds who enjoy interacting with their owners.

THE LILAC-CROWNED AMAZON

The Lilac-crowned Amazon, also known as Finsch's Amazon, is sometimes confused with the Mexican Red-head as the latter has a small lilac-colored area near the eyes and ear coverts. If you compare

Mexican Red-head Amazon

the photos of these two parrots, you will notice that on the Lilac-crown almost the entire crown and nape are lilac colored. In addition, the marking between its eyes is a deep maroon color, which in the Red-head is a bright red.

The Lilac-crown has limited speech potential and it was not imported into the United States in great numbers. Some breeding stock does exist and is providing chicks for those who seek this parrot.

Lilac-crowned Amazons

MEALY AMAZONS

Mealy Amazons are members of a group of large stocky parrots with fairly subdued colors. They are green parrots whose markings vary widely and include yellow markings on the forehead and blue markings on the crown. Their white eye-ring gives them a comical appearance that is often matched by their behavior. Mealy and Blue-crowned Amazons are members of the same group and show similar characteristics. They have limited speech skills but make enjoyable, playful and friendly pets.

Mealy Amazon

African Greys

African Greys are among the most popular parrots kept in the United States today. They meet the basic requirements for popularity in that they are available as domestic babies and their price (about $1,000) is not totally prohibitive.

I remember the keen excitement I felt when I arrived to pick up my first African Grey from a lady who was selling him because he and her dog failed to interact peacefully. He was out on a perch when I arrived and even though his owner cautioned me not to try to touch him, I was drawn to the parrot as if by a powerful magnet. I slowly held out my hand and

African Grey

the little Grey climbed right on and started to nibble my thumb. The result was an immediate sale and a great deal of pleasure for me. This bird had been hand-fed as a baby and easily transferred his interest and affection from one owner to another.

Many owners have said that African Greys have a greater tendency to pluck their feathers than other parrots, and there seems to be some truth to this. It is possible that with their high intelligence African Greys experience greater frustration than other parrots when ignored or left alone. If you own a Grey, keep him happy and occupied and give him the attention he craves. The African Grey delights in objects he can manipulate or take apart as well as a good deal of attention from his owners.

If you want a parrot to cuddle and roughhouse with, the Grey is not a perfect choice. Most of them tend to spook easily and will shy away from your hand even when they are tame and friendly. Tame Greys will endure your holding and petting them but it is not something they appear to enjoy in the way that Amazons, cockatoos and macaws do.

Many African Greys are bred in the United States on a regular basis. It should not be hard for you to find a pet shop or breeder within traveling distance, so you can choose one after watching it play and after having had a chance to interact with it. (This, of course, is the best way to purchase any parrot.)

THE CONGO GREY

African Greys, of course, originally came from Africa. The most common and most widely kept Grey is the so-called Congo Grey, which is a name commonly applied to any large African Grey whether it comes from the Congo region or not.

Congo Grey

The Congo Grey is a small parrot that reaches lengths of about thirteen to fourteen inches. The upper surface of the body is a visibly darker gray than the under surface. They have a shiny black beak and a bright red tail. Greys less than a year old have a dark iris that turns to yellow as they mature. If you are being offered a baby Grey, make sure the eye is dark.

Congo Greys can develop an excellent vocabulary, and when they do learn to talk it is with the voice and inflections of those who teach them. Greys can cause confusion by sounding like their owners or even like another animal in the household. Their voices are quite different than that of other parrots, who tend to screech what they have to say. Unfortunately not every African Grey will learn to talk. If you purchase an older bird of two or three years of age and it is not talking, it probably never will speak. Those who are talented talkers will learn new words and phrases throughout their lives and provide a constant source of amusement for their owners and visitors.

Timneh Grey

THE TIMNEH GREY

A close relative to the Congo Grey, the Timneh Grey is several inches smaller and has a pinkish beak along with a maroon-colored tail. These parrots are as talented as the Congo Grey, sell for slightly less money and should be considered for purchase as they make fine pets.

Macaws

Macaws make wonderful pets. They are clever and can be taught to do simple tricks and sometimes fairly complex ones. Tame macaws love to play and roughhouse with their owners. They love having their cheeks rubbed and their necks scratched. I once owned a giant Scarlet Macaw who even liked having his tongue scratched.

Of course, there are some drawbacks. These large parrots can produce very loud screams. These are not screams of anger—just morning and evening yells announcing that the day has started or that they want company or wish to be fed. They also require a good-size cage, which will take up a lot of room. All parrots should be housed in roomy cages, and in the case of the macaws, it is important that they be given plenty of out-of-cage play time. It is cruel to keep a large parrot in its cage at all times. Macaws respond to being out of their cages by vigorous wing flapping and athletic endeavors such as swinging and hanging by their beaks, antics that are delightful to watch.

Although they are capable of limited speech, macaws are not great talkers. The words or phrases that they utter are usually quite loud and somewhat distorted.

The Blue and Gold Macaw

The Blue and Gold Macaw has a largely blue upper surface and tail. The neck and chest are a bright yellow while the cheeks have a black band that runs down to

Blue and Gold Macaw

the chin. The crown and forehead are green while the white cheeks are accentuated by rows of black feathers, giving these macaws the appearance a painted savage. The large black beak is quite powerful and capable of cracking nuts, chewing wood or destroying toys. These large birds easily reach lengths of thirty-two to thirty-three inches at maturity.

The Blue and Gold is the most commonly kept macaw because of its availability, beautiful colors and fine disposition. These characteristics also make them favorites at shows like Parrot Jungle or Busch Gardens, where these remarkable birds are taught to perform clever tricks, including riding on bicycles or solving simple puzzles.

43

THE SCARLET MACAW

The Scarlet Macaw is almost as popular as the Blue and Gold, but because female Scarlets always seem to be in short supply there are not as many Scarlets offered for sale as Blue and Golds.

The Scarlet Macaw's feathers are a rich mix of red, blue and yellow with some green markings and a large bare cheek. Its upper beak is horn colored while the lower beak is dark black. It is about the same size as the Blue and Gold Macaw and its habits and disposition are quite similar.

There have been cases of inbreeding between Scarlets and Blue and Gold Macaws with the resulting offspring having a mix of both bird's characteristics. This type of hybridization is unwise as it serves no purpose and produces offspring that will not breed true for the characteristics of either parent.

Scarlet Macaw

GREEN-WINGED MACAW

The Green-winged Macaw is often confused with the Scarlet as it also has a large area of red and blue feathers. It is easy to differentiate between them if you remember that the Green-winged Macaw has a horn-colored upper beak with a black tip and a black lower beak. In addition it has an attractive design of bright red feather lines on its cheek. The Green Wing is also a few inches larger than the Scarlet.

Green-winged Macaws are not as easy to locate as Blue and Gold or Scarlet Macaws because they were not imported as frequently and their importa-

tion was ended even before the implementation of the laws that stopped the importation of all exotic birds.

Their behavior, temperament, talking skills and other characteristics are very similar to those of the macaws described above.

MILITARY MACAW

The Military Macaw, about twenty-eight inches long, is not as colorful as the Scarlet, Blue and Gold or Green Wing. It is a dark olive green except for a clump of bright red feathers that look as if they were pasted to its forehead. Its white cheek areas have a delicate tracing of greenish-black feathers. Military Macaws reach lengths of twenty-seven to twenty-eight inches.

Green-winged Macaw

They are less common than the macaws mentioned above, but if you have the opportunity to own one do not pass it up as they make friendly and interesting pets.

THE HYACINTH MACAW

This parrot seems to be the dream bird for most people who wish to own a macaw. These beautiful parrots can be as large as forty inches. They have a striking appearance as their deep blue feathers are set off with bright yellow markings around the eye and on the cheek.

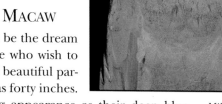

Military Macaw

45

As is true of many large parrots, Hyacinth Macaws are gentle and confident even when handled by strangers. I recommend respectful treatment if you do get to hold one, as their beaks are extremely powerful. It is quite an experience, however, to be offered the chance to have forty inches of warm, live parrot sit on your shoulder as it nuzzles your hair or ear.

Hyacinth Macaw

Hyacinth Macaws are quite expensive; hand-fed babies sell for 7,000 to 8,000 dollars. In spite of their size and original rarity there are many breeding pairs in the United States that regularly produce healthy chicks. If you have the money, space and desire you can own this outstanding parrot.

MINIATURE MACAWS

The name miniature macaws is given to a group of smaller parrots that include the Severe, Yellow-collared, Hahns, Noble, Illigers and Red-bellied Macaws. This group ranges in size from twelve to twenty inches. Although they are not particularly common, they do appear on the market occasionally. With the exception of the Yellow-collared, they have limited speech skills, though in many ways they look and act like their larger relatives. Owning a mini-macaw may be the answer for someone who lacks the space to keep a full-size macaw.

Cockatoos

When I first became interested in parrots I enjoyed reading a book that described a Greater Sulphur Cockatoo named Tommy, shown with his owner in a delightful photograph with the bird comfortably nestled in his owner's sweater and only his head sticking out. After owning cockatoos for more than twenty years I can say that this photograph epitomizes cockatoo behavior.

Hahns Macaw

This photo also inspired me to search for a baby Greater. When I finally located one about three months old, I rushed to purchase it. One of my fondest memories is spoon-feeding her from a jar of baby food. Even though she was already fully weaned, she was more than willing to engage in this tasty charade. Although cockatoos are low on the list of talented talking parrots, they can speak and I have found that the little they say is often appropriate. They are parrots with endearing personality traits who love to be the center of attention. To get this attention they will engage in all sorts of dramatic moves with their heads and bodies twisting and turning in the most bizarre manner.

There are great tales about the long lives of cockatoos. Life spans of forty or fifty years are not unusual, and cockatoos whose diet and exercise sessions are carefully maintained can live even longer, though stories of cockatoos who lived a hundred or more years are generally apocryphal. King Tut, who was presented to the San Diego Zoo by explorer Frank Buck in 1925, is an example of an authenticated case of cockatoos' longevity. He lived until 1991.

THE GREAT SULPHUR-CRESTED COCKATOO

The Greater Sulphur-crested Cockatoo is a white parrot about nineteen inches long. It has a bright yellow crest that it erects when angry, startled or excited, and a wash of yellow feathers on its cheeks, ears and under the surface of the wings and tail. Its beak is large and jet black.

This delightful parrot can be found in several varieties. The most common of these are the "true" Greater, descended from birds imported from Australia, and the Triton, which originated in New Guinea and which has a blue eye-ring. Other than the blue eye-ring there is no difference between the two parrots and their behavior and skills are identical. Triton babies sell for less than true Greaters because there are more of them available. This is because no Greaters have been legally exported from Australia since the mid-1960s.

The Greater is a highly intelligent bird who loves to interact with its owners. If you plan to purchase one you should be sure that you or members of your family will have time to spend with this cockatoo, as it suffers when it doesn't get enough attention. To some degree, this is true of all the full-size parrots.

Greater Sulphur-crested Cockatoo

LESSER SULPHUR-CRESTED COCKATOOS

Lesser Sulphur-crested Cockatoos make up a group of small versions of the above-mentioned bird. Their average size is about thirteen inches, which makes them easier to house than the Greater. This group includes the most common Lesser, a stocky bird with a broad beak and a thick crest, and the Citron-crested, which is slightly larger than the Lesser and has an orange-hued crest. These are clever and amiable parrots whose energetic activity makes them a pleasure to watch. As with the larger cockatoos, a good deal of their performance is directed at their human audience

Citron-crested (on left) and Lesser Sulphur-crested Cockatoos

and they will often get wilder and wilder if their audience shows signs of leaving. Speaking is not among the top skills of the Lesser Cockatoos, but they are capable of mimicry as well as some unclear mutterings.

MOLUCCAN COCKATOOS

Moluccan Cockatoos are large, noisy parrots that come in various shades of pink and white. The more deeply colored birds are highly desired. Their backward-curving, salmon-colored crest is quite attractive but not too obvious until it is held erect. Mature birds are about twenty inches long, although they appear larger when they raise their crests.

They are wonderful acrobats and their energetic performances make them amusing to observe. Keep in mind, however, that these cockatoos have extremely loud calls and it can be quite startling if you happen to be close by when they scream, particularly if your back is turned to them. Be cautious about obtaining one if your housing situation means that loud morning and evening screams cannot be tolerated.

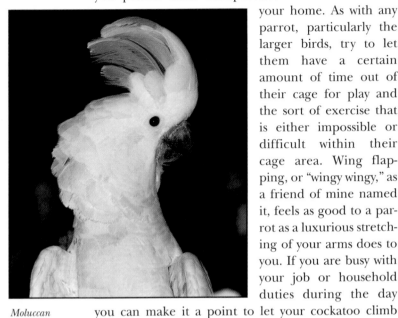

Moluccans have a propensity for chewing, and their large beaks are capable of serious destruction if you permit them unsupervised access to areas of your home. As with any parrot, particularly the larger birds, try to let them have a certain amount of time out of their cage for play and the sort of exercise that is either impossible or difficult within their cage area. Wing flapping, or "wingy wingy," as a friend of mine named it, feels as good to a parrot as a luxurious stretching of your arms does to you. If you are busy with your job or household duties during the day

Moluccan Cockatoo

you can make it a point to let your cockatoo climb out of his cage while you are doing your evening cleanup or preparing dinner. If he is as greedy as my birds, once you have put his food dish back into his cage he'll willingly climb back in to sample the goodies.

THE UMBRELLA COCKATOO

This parrot is sometimes confused with the Moluccan because it's just an inch or two smaller. Both parrots share the features of a black beak and a large crest. The Umbrella, however, is a white parrot with just a wash of yellow on the underside of its wings and tail. The crest is so tall that

Umbrella Cockatoo

this cockatoo provides a comical appearance of surprise and astonishment when its large white crest is raised.

THE BARE-EYED COCKATOO

The Bare-eyed Cockatoo, a fourteen- to fifteen-inch dynamo of activity, chatter and mischief, is not partic-ularly handsome but is very bright. These white birds have pink and yellow markings as well as an oddly shaped, asymmetrical blue eye-ring that extends further below the eye than it does at the top or sides. It has a fairly small beak and its crest is so meager that unless lifted in excitement, you do not realize it exists.

Unlike most of the other cockatoos, the Bare-eyed is an excellent mimic and talker, and most parrot fanciers rate it as the best talker among the cockatoos. It also demonstrates a high level of intelligence and friendli-ness. I have seen several who, when permitted to walk about the bird room, followed their owner around while gently pulling at her shoelaces.

Bare-eyed Cockatoo

GOFFIN'S COCKATOO

The Goffin's Cockatoo is a close relative of the Bare-eyed. Its native habitat is the Tenimbar Islands. Starting in 1972, the level of agricultural activities as well as deforesting on these islands destroyed much of the cockatoo's habitat, and the loss of their tree-sheltered areas made them highly vulnerable to capture. Since this period coincided with the opening of the quarantine stations set up in the United States, huge numbers of Goffins were exported. The diminished numbers in their home islands are some-what compensated for by the large number of pairs breeding in the United States and Europe.

Goffin's Cockatoo

The Goffin lacks the blue eye-ring of the Bare-eyed but, other than that and a slightly smaller build, it is essentially the same. The Goffin sells for somewhat less than the Bare-eyed and should definitely be considered as a pet if you are offered a tame, hand-fed baby. Goffins are just as talented and clever as the Bare-eyed although some owners may consider them (and the Bare-eyed) too clever, as these parrots are experts at escaping from their cages. If you decide to own either, be sure to lock your cage door with a closing device that will defy their skills as master escapists.

ROSE-BREASTED COCKATOO

The Rose-breasted Cockatoo, or Galah, as it is known in its native Australia, is a fourteen-inch-long, beauti-fully colored pink and gray parrot with a tiny crest and a small beak. It is despised in its homeland because of the damage it does to fruit and vegetable crops. But, although farmers attempt to drive them off and worse, these birds are so clever and likable that many farmers also keep them as pets.

Rose-breasted Cockatoos are bred with great success in the United States and Europe, where they are very popular birds. A friend who visited me after picking up her newly acquired baby Rose-breasted at the airport sang to the bird as he stood on our dining room table and gazed with interest at the group of humans who were peering at him. Within seconds the little cockatoo began to dance from side to side in time to the singing of her new owner.

Rose-breasted Cockatoos

Eclectus

Although the eclectus has been known as a pet for many years, it is only relatively recently that it became truly popular. Prior to the late 1980s, rumors about their frailty and difficult behavior tended to discourage ownership of these sleek and colorful birds. Some of the rumors stemmed from some importers' ignorance of proper diet for their newly acquired stock. A special feeding regimen and attention would have helped the newcomers to adjust. The eclectus available today are all domestically bred birds and diet is no longer a problem as they do well on the standard seed or pellet diet along with a good supply of vegetables and fruits.

The lure of the eclectus is partially based on their specialized feathering. The structures that make up their feathers are so tightly entwined that a clean, healthy eclectus appears to be covered with hair or fur rather than feathers. Males are a lush green with reddish wing markings while females are a grand mix of green, lavender and red, giving the impression of being robed like royalty. Even more so than other parrots, eclectus look their best when their feathers are kept clean, so frequent spraying with tepid water during mild weather or warm periods of the day is an important part of their general care.

A female eclectus

Another aspect of their popularity stems from their congenial and responsive behavior. Some parrots can be lavished with affection and show a minimum of return. This is not true of the eclectus, who will repay your love measure for measure. In addition, eclectus are not noisy unless something unusual stimulates them to respond with a screech.

There are ten major types of eclectus. In all of them the males are green with some reddish markings and the females are green with markings that may include red, blue, maroon and lavender. There are also small size differences among the groups. The Solomon Island Eclectus is said to be most amenable to taming and training, but I have known Vosmaeri, Grand Eclectus, Red-sided and even Cornelia's Eclectus to be just as pleasant. If you decide to purchase an eclectus parrot as a pet, choose based on health and tameness rather than which particular subspecies it is.

Lories and Lorikeets

Lories and lorikeets are very similar parrots. The lories have shorter tails and are somewhat larger than the lorikeets, but both groups exhibit the same interesting, active and playful behavior and are a delight to watch.

They are a somewhat specialized group of parrots, and for many years were kept only by experts who had the time, knowledge and facilities to deal with these brightly colored, quick-moving parrots. Lories and lorikeets have very special dietary needs because in the wild they feed mainly on fruits, nectar and pollen. Their tongues are modified for this type of diet. Keeping in mind the old adage that "you are what you eat," it is obvious that the droppings of this family are liquid and particularly messy. In recent years the development of special lory diets has modified this situation to a degree. That, along with the development of suspended, easy-to-clean cages, makes it possible for more people to own these intensely colored birds.

Red Lory

The suspended cages are open on all six sides, including the bottom, and thus they can be thoroughly hosed down when necessary. Of course, you could not keep this type of cage in your living room, but if you really want to keep a lory or lorikeet, an appropriate housing spot can be found in many homes.

Many of the lories are excellent breeders in captivity and this makes it possible for you to own the more

55

common ones at reasonable prices. One of the best known lories is the Blue-streaked, which, because of the arrangement and color of its feathers, gives the illusion of having blue streaks on it back and neck. The ear coverings are blue and it also has black and red markings. It is a magnificently colored parrot.

Other typical members of the family include the Red Lory, which has bright red colors with blue

markings under the tail and around the vent. This is set off by a deep orange beak. The Black and Purple-capped Lory, whose name describes its most outstanding marking, is also quite popular.

The lorikeet I find the most attractive is the Blue Mountain Lorikeet, also known as Swainson's Lorikeet. Its head and abdomen are

Ornate Lory

a deep blue and it also exhibits a yellowish-green collar and a scarlet and yellow breast. Many of these beauties have been bred in captivity and are available as pets.

Conures

There are many reasons to chose a conure as your parrot pet. Many types are abundant, they are less expensive than most of the full-size parrots and they are fun to watch and play with. In virtually every respect other than size, they look and act like their larger relatives, the Amazons. As with most smaller parrots, they have a very limited vocabulary and a shrill, penetrating call. This can become annoying if it continues unabated, but access to toys or playing tapes or a radio will generally entertain them enough to reduce their screams and whistles to a tolerable degree. Keep in mind that when you buy a parrot of any type you certainly aren't expecting to get a silent bird. Conures are wonderful chewers and you should provide them with plenty of small sticks or wooden blocks on which they can demonstrate this skill.

Markings on most of the members of the conure group are highly variable so several characteristics should be used when trying to identify one.

Sun Conure

The Sun Conure

The Sun Conure is one of the most popular conures. It is about twelve inches long and a bright yellow color with a mixture of orange, blue and green markings. It has a brownish-colored eye set in a white eye-ring and a shiny black beak.

Jenday Conures

Jenday Conures are about the same size as the Sun Conures and have a bright yellow head, neck and abdomen. Their blue-black flight feathers and blue-tipped tails along with green markings make this a very colorful parrot. They also have a black beak. They are similar to the Sun Conure in many ways and some authorities believe them to be closely related. Because both groups breed readily, the two should be kept separate so that hybrid breeding does not occur.

Jenday Conures

Jendays are quite playful and, if obtained as youngsters, will develop a strong and loving bond with their owner. Watching a cage full of young Jendays can be as enjoyable as looking at a group of puppies in a pet shop.

HALFMOON CONURES

Halfmoons are probably the most well-known conure as they have been written about and kept as pets for more than a hundred years. They are also known as Petz's Conures and Orange-fronted Conures, but the more mellifluous Halfmoon name is most commonly used in the United States.

The fame of the Halfmoon stems partially from its good nature and willingness to interact in a friendly manner with its owner. Of course, the fact that these ten-inch-long parrots have always been available has also enhanced their popularity. The Halfmoon is a green bird with an orange marking on its forehead and crown that blends into blue toward the rear of the head. These birds are so clever and agile that they have been frequently used in parrot shows and on occasion in television commercials.

A similarly marked relative, the Peach-fronted or Gold-crowned Conure is frequently confused with the Halfmoon. One easy way to distinguish between the two is to remember that the Halfmoon has a beak that is yellowish-white while that of the Peach-fronted is black. In all other respects they are remarkably similar.

QUEEN OF BAVARIA CONURE

We have taken care to cover the types of parrots that would normally be available to you in pet shops or from breeders. The Queen of Bavaria Conure is an excep-

Halfmoon Conure

tion. This is a striking bird that reaches a length of fourteen inches. This size along with its massive beak makes this parrot look like some sort of unusual Amazon to those unaware of just which parrot they are looking at. Their brilliant yellow feathers have earned them the nickname of "Golden Conure." (Though some fanciers have said that this could refer to their price, as a single bird may sell for thousands of dollars.) They also have green flight feathers. Extensive variation in markings is typical of this group, and chicks from the same clutch even show different markings.

Permits are required to purchase these conures, but even with a permit they are so rare, costly and endangered that it would be ethical to purchase them only if you intended to breed them.

59

THE NANDAY CONURE

The Nanday Conure is a fairly noisy twelve-inch conure with a black beak and black head. Because of slight differences in body structure, it is considered to be in a separate group from the conures mentioned previously. These parrots breed freely and have always been accessible as pets.

PATAGONIAN CONURE

The Patagonian Conure is another Conure, grouped differently than the birds described in the preceding pages.

Patagonians appear much larger than most other conures but this is because of their long, tapering tail that can extend their total length to sixteen to seventeen inches. Their major color is olive green, which appears on the back, head and neck, while their abdomen is yellow. They are very loud birds but breed freely and are worth considering if you decide to try your hand at parrot breeding.

Ringnecks and Their Relatives

Various types of Ringneck parrots make up an interesting group of birds referred to as "Psittacula." These long-tailed birds are referred to as parakeets as well as parrots. Do not confuse them with the small budgies of Australia; they are not related.

The Ringnecks originated in Asia and Africa and are larger and have much longer tails than the Australian budgies. Some fanciers refer to the entire group as the "long-tailed parrots." In addition to long tails, members of this group have large heads and beaks giving them a somewhat top-heavy look.

The **Alexandrine Parakeet** is the largest of the group as it reaches lengths of twenty to twenty-two inches. This impressive-looking bird has a large, red, powerful beak. Its body color is green with a tinge of blue on the cheeks. They also have a wide black neck-ring that becomes pink at the nape of the neck. This marking provides their alternative name of Rose-ringed Parakeet. Females lack the ring and also have shorter tail feathers.

Alexandrines have a friendly nature and make good pets. Beware, however, of their ability to destroy wood and even thin cage wire. Cages and flights for these birds should be heavily reinforced.

The **African Ringneck** is a green parrot with a light green under surface. It is about fourteen inches long with the tail feathers making up much of its length. It has a deep red upper beak with a black tip. Its black ring becomes pink as it reaches the nape of the neck.

Indian Ringneck

The **Indian Ringneck** is much more commonly kept than the African and about an inch larger. It is a light green with a yellowish undersurface. This parrot's collar markings are a deeper color than the African and its beak is also larger. The upper beak is a dark red while the lower portion is black.

They are energetic parrots that frequently produce mutations with fabulous color variations. Breeders of Ringnecks make every effort to stabilize these color variations so that they can eventually breed true. The normal Indian Ringneck sells for moderate prices, but the rare color varieties are much more expensive.

The **Mustache Parakeet** is an aptly named member of the Ringnecks. At thirteen inches in length it is slightly smaller than the birds just described. Its head is gray with a tinge of pale blue that meets the green nape. In males the upper beak is a bright red and the lower a brownish black. Adult males have a black neck ring which reaches from the lower beak to the ear coverts and resembles a large mustache.

The **Slaty-headed Parakeet** is about fifteen inches long and is distinguished by its bluish gray head. This becomes darker at the neck and eventually forms a black collar or ring. They have a red upper beak with a yellow tip and a yellow lower beak. In females the head is a lighter color.

Lovebirds

This interesting group of small parrots is poorly named as the birds tend to be pugnacious with their own species and aggressive with other birds or strange humans. In spite of this they are very popular as pets because their prolific breed-ing keeps them regularly avail-able at reasonable prices. In addition, many individuals enjoy working with the com-monly occurring mutations in an effort to "fix" these varia-tions so that they will breed true in the future.

Peach-faced Lovebird

The **Black-Collared Lovebird,** also known as Swinderin's Lovebird, is about five inches long and is green with a black collar on the neck. The upper abdomen has an orange-yellow band. The beak is black and the eyes are yellow.

Fischer's Lovebirds

The **Abyssinian Lovebird** is larger than six inches. Males are green with a red forehead, beak and eye-ring. In females the colors are muted and the eye-ring is absent.

63

The **Red-faced Lovebird** is more commonly available then the three lovebirds described above. It is about five and a half inches long with a face, forehead and neck marked in bright red. Because the red does not completely cover the area to the rear of the eyes, the contrast between the green head and the red face creates the illusion of a bright mask. This parrot has a red upper beak and an orange lower beak. Females have lighter colors and an orange face instead of a red one.

The **Madagascar Lovebird** is also called the Gray-headed Lovebird. It is a bit longer than five inches. Males have a gray head, neck, throat and upper abdomen while in hens, these regions are green. The beak in males is horn colored while the female's is yellow.

Masked Lovebird

The **Peach-faced Lovebird** is the best known and most commonly kept of the lovebirds, and is also the largest of the group. Males have a reddish-pink forehead, throat, cheeks, chin and upper abdomen. The rest of their body is a bright green. Females tend to have muted colors and are slightly larger than males.

The **Black-cheeked Lovebird** is almost six inches long and has a brownish-black forehead and cheeks. The sides and rear of the head are a yellowish-green while the throat is orange. There is also a pink marking on the chest. The female's colors are not as bright.

The **Nyasa Lovebird** is four and a half inches long with a bright red forehead and crown. The throat and cheeks are orange-red while the rest of the plumage is green. It also has a bright red beak. The female has slightly duller colors.

Fischer's Lovebird is another extremely popular parrot about six inches long. It is largely green with a yellow neck marking. Its cheeks and throat are orange. The head is green with a bright red marking on the forehead. These birds breed freely in captivity.

The **Masked Lovebird** is about six and a half inches long. Its head is brownish black with a yellow collar. The throat and chest are orange. It also has a large white eye-ring and a red beak. They breed freely and produce fascinating mutations such as the Blue Masked Lovebird.

Caiques

Caiques (rhymes with "likes") are small, playful, birds with short, squared-off tails. In many ways they resemble the conures. They are about ten inches long and although their speech is limited and their calls are shrill, many people find that watching a pair tumble and play together can be the best part of their day.

A pair of Black-headed Caiques

The popular **Black-headed Caique** is a ten-inch-long bird who looks as if he is wearing a black cap pulled down over his eyes. The region below the cap is a light green and the abdomen and belly are white.

The **White-bellied Caique** is sometimes referred to as the White-breasted Caique. It is about nine inches long and has an orange head. The abdomen and belly are a clean white.

These little parrots can be obtained at reasonable prices and make excellent pets. If you are new to parrots, they are a good bird for you to begin with.

Living
with

part three

Your
Parrot

chapter 4

Your Parrot's Home

Green-winged Macaw

Now you have chosen the right bird for your family and lifestyle. Before you bring it home, there are a few things you should do to prepare for your new pet.

Housing

How you house your parrot is an important decision that should be made even before you bring your new pet home. Try to avoid the use of a temporary cage as this means an additional step in adjustment when you move the bird from one cage to the other. Purchase an airline travel kennel in which to transport the parrot to your house, and have his cage ready and waiting for him when he arrives. If you have purchased the parrot from an out-of-town breeder be sure that they ship him to you in a safe and comfortable travel kennel.

When choosing the cage remember that your bird will spend much of his time in it. The size and shape of the cage you choose should, of course, be determined by the size and, to a certain extent, the configuration of the parrot. Large parrots with long tails, like macaws, will be more comfortable in rectangular cages that are tall enough to keep their tails from rubbing the bottom of the cage when they are sitting on their perch. Large cockatoos do not need the height to protect their tails but will enjoy it anyway because they love to climb and swing. Avoid the highly decorative but impractical domed or peaked cages as these deprive the parrots of a surface on which they can swing and climb. It's important that the cage feels good to the bird, not that it looks good in your living room. The *minimum*-size cage for a full-size macaw or cockatoo should be at least three to four square feet.

A big parrot with a long tail, like this Catalina Macaw, needs a large, tall cage.

The cage you choose for your parrot depends on his size— generally, the larger the cage, the better.

If you can't find one like this at a realistic price consider making one yourself. It's a fairly simple construction project. Cage wire and other supplies are available through ads in various bird magazines. Remember that macaws and cockatoos, as well as many other full-size parrots, require heavy-gauge cage wire or they will be able to flex and break it over a period of time.

Parrots such as Amazons, African Greys and conures should have a cage at least two feet by two feet by thirty inches and a larger cage would be even better.

Baby birds, like this young African Grey, have yet to become fully coordinated.

On many occasions you will see the terms *flight* or *aviary* used in books and articles about parrots. A flight is a large enclosure usually used for one of more pairs of birds and is ideal for breeding parrots. If you have the space a flight can be built indoors or, if your climate permits, it can be located out of doors. One or more parrots living in a flight will have excellent opportunities for exercise and play. In addition, their activities will be so engaging to watch that you might want to consider building a flight as an adjacent structure to your living room. The term *aviary* is used to described one or more flights. Aviaries are almost always devoted to breeding birds.

Perches

You will probably need to buy the perches separate from the cage. Provide several places in his cage where the bird can stand comfortably on two feet. Varying the perches' thickness and texture makes the bird's cage a more interesting environment.

If you have brought home a baby bird he may still be unable to exercise his full array of climbing skills. To avoid falls or frustration, provide several perches at low levels and keep the seed and water cups at the same level as one of these until the young parrot has demonstrated he can climb freely. This should not take more than a few weeks.

Cage Cover

A heavy cloth draped over a bird's cage seems to calm him down and signal "nighttime." It will also protect him from drafts during the night. Make sure you choose a washable fabric.

Seed and Water Cups

Your new parrot's cage must be equipped with water and seed containers. Inexpensive cages frequently come with small plastic dishes held in place with a clamp that you flip up when you want to remove the dish. These are far from ideal; even a small parrot can chew them. They are also hard to keep clean, and are easy for the parrot to remove and drop to the floor.

Ceramic seed and water dishes are best because they are heavy and a mischievous parrot cannot tip them over. (Yellow-naped Amazon)

Smart parrots usually do this when the dishes are full and will make the greatest mess. If you must use this type of cage cup, obtain the glass substitute as they are much easier to clean, fit more tightly and your parrot will probably not be able to remove them.

You can also try other dishes that do not make use of the existing clamp. These attach inside the cage with various devices. Some of the better arrangements have quick-release

71

clamps that you can open but the parrot cannot. The one disadvantage to these is that you will have to open the cage and put your hands inside to take dishes out and replace them. This will not be a problem for you but if circumstances require someone else to feed your parrot, they may not be as happy to do this.

A variety of commercial and homemade toys are available to keep your parrot stimulated and happy.

The seed and water dishes I prefer are the hooded type which fit into metal holders attached to the inside of the cage. These are made of china so they can be cleaned in your dishwasher and come in and out of their brackets fairly easily. They are also quite heavy so the average parrot will not be able to lift them out to drop to the cage floor. The hooded design prevents droppings from entering the cups and this avoids contamination of the seeds and water.

Do not put seed or water dishes on the floor of the cage. The contents will quickly become fouled if you do, and the birds will think nothing of stepping in and out of the dishes to add to the general lack of sanitary conditions.

PARROT SUPPLIES

You will need the following supplies for your parrot:

Cage of appropriate size

At least one perch

Safe toys

Food and water dishes

Cloth for cage cover

Spray bottle

High quality seed mix or pelleted food

Parrot Toys

Your new parrot also needs toys to keep him happy and entertained. Parrots are playful animals who enjoy challenging activities. They also enjoy using their beaks and claws. Keep these personality traits in mind when you choose your parrot's toys.

Do not make the mistake of filling the cage with too many toys or other items. Doing so will crowd the bird and make it difficult for you to work with him if you have to reach into the cage to encourage him to come out. At these times, toys become objects for the parrot to cling to so that you cannot easily get him to come out.

Toys need not be expensive or complicated. Parrots enjoy items that can be chewed and also take pleasure in swinging items in their cage so that they hit the sides of the cage to make noise. Something as simple as a block of unstained wood (pine is excellent) can be drilled and hung from a leather thong for the parrot to chew, swing from and also push back and forth. Make sure that the thong is wide enough so that it cannot form a noose and that the leather is untreated, as your eager parrot will probably chew the leather as well as the wood. If he seems unable to get a good chewing grip on the wood, drill a number of holes through it and he will find it more satisfying. Don't worry about how rapidly he destroys the wood as pine scraps are either free or inexpensive.

This Rose-breasted Cockatoo is enjoying chewing on a thick leather thong.

If you have a willow tree available to you it is easy to cut three- or four-inch lengths from the branches that you trim during the spring and summer. These make excellent chewing toys. Use pruning shears to cut pieces of willow with a dia-meter of about half an inch. This size can be easily gripped by the parrot as he rips off the outer bark and then crunches the rest of the twig to splinters. Cutting anything much thicker than half an inch with pruning shears is quite a challenge, so stick to the smaller size.

Thread spools, and other objects of untreated wood, make great chewing toys for parrots. (Lilac-crowned Amazon)

For many years I collected wooden spools from sewing thread and also purchased packages of wooden clothespins for my birds. The spools were perfect as they were clean pine with a hole drilled through the middle. They could easily be hung from a leather thong and chewed to bits even by small parrots. Unfortunately they have been replaced by plastic and cardboard thread holders. Wooden clothespins were perfect toys as they were also clean pine and could be wedged on a cage bar or hung from a leather thong. Their spring-loaded descendants have no value as toys. If you can find some of these old-fashioned accessories, save them for parrot toys!

Like many parrots, these two climbed on top of their cage as soon as they were let out. (Yellow-fronted Amazons)

Tongue depressors used by doctors are also great. Leather craft shops very often have large quantities of scrap leather available in varying thicknesses. Ask to purchase a supply of any scraps that are untreated or unstained. These can be cut into smaller pieces and make wonderful and safe chewing toys. Large pieces that are not too thick can be cut into strips (at least half an inch wide) and used to hang other toys.

One company makes a hard rubber toy with interesting shapes. These toys can be bitten, swung or pulled at by your parrot. I've never actually seen one torn apart, though, and they come in sizes to suit parrots of any size.

Bells are also great fun for parrots but make sure that you get a large one with a clapper that is not made of lead and that cannot be removed. If necessary, wire the clapper in yourself using a technique that will prevent your parrot from getting it out. Small cowbells are usually ideal and you can purchase them at a farm supply store.

SWINGS

Some parrots enjoy swings and others just use them as another perch. I don't recommend the swings that come with cages as they are usually much too small, and if the parrot is foolish enough to use it he will wind up sitting in a hunched-over position.

You can make your own swing by cutting a length of three-quarter-inch dowel and then drilling a hole in each end that is slightly smaller than an eighth of an inch. Obtain one-eighth-inch-diameter copper rods at the hardware store and bend the rods to fit loosely over the top cage wires. After you have done your bending, push the rods through the holes and then tap them with a mallet to deform the ends so that

CAGE SET-UP

Make sure the cage is large enough for your parrot to have a minimum amount of room to stretch his wings and fly (remember that birds fly horizontally). The larger the bird, the larger the cage he will need. For a larger parrot, the cage should be tall enough so the bird's tail does not touch the bottom while he is sitting on the perch. Larger parrots—like cockatoos and macaws—require a great deal of cage space; if you cannot comfortably provide this amount of room, consider getting one of the smaller parrot species instead.

The cage should contain perches, toys, food and water dishes. Place the perch or perches at a medium height, and provide a few choice toys for the bird to play with. Don't put in too many toys as this will only overwhelm the bird.

To keep food and water dishes from becoming contaminated, place them on the side of the cage away from the perch.

Line the inside of the cage with newspaper and change this daily.

Place the cage in a location out of direct drafts and sunlight, in a place where your bird will be safe from loud noises and household commotion.

they will pull out of the wood. When you install the swing make sure it does not interfere with the parrot's access to his seed or water dishes and that it doesn't block him from reaching his perches. If you want to keep it fixed in one place use pliers to squeeze the bends closed. I leave mine open far enough so that the swing can be slid from one side to the other.

Sophisticated toys such as music boxes and tape recorders that are foot activated also exist, but I think they are probably more pleasing to the owner than the parrot.

PARROT GYMS

Most parrots will climb to the top of their cages if you leave their cage door open. They will then play on the top as

Make sure the toys you offer your parrot are safe and sturdy. (Moluccan Cockatoo)

well as climbing down the sides and back up again. Simple gyms are on the market that can be attached to the top of the cage to make it more interesting. These are inexpensive, but it may be better for your parrot to be off a perch and on the cage wires for a period of time.

Whether you choose toys that are commercially produced or homemade, always keep safety in mind.

chapter 5

Feeding
Your
Parrot

I'll never forget the day I visited Blondi II, a Double-yellow Head that I ultimately purchased. He lived in a good-size cage in the back bedroom of a small house. His original owner had died and the gentleman's widow had little time for the bird as she was working out of the  home for the first time in many years. Because their grown children were away at college, this once beloved pet was now given very little attention. An obvious indication of this was the way in which the hulls of his daily ration of sunflower seeds formed a small, peaked mountain at the bottom of his cage just below his food dish. The owner would rush into Blondi's room, fill his cup with seeds, provide fresh water and then she was off again. Not much of a life for Blondi and certainly not much of a diet.

Hyacinth Macaw

Feeding the Proper Diet

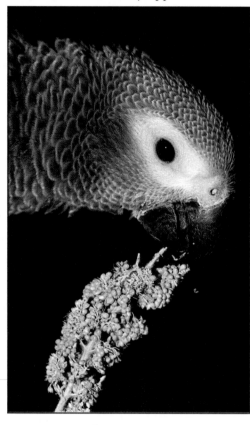

The day of the sunflower and peanut diet is long gone. Excellent pelleted provisions as well as fine seed mixes are commonly available in pet shops or by mail. When I first began keeping parrots a typical diet included sunflower seed, safflower seed, millet, cracked corn, hemp, oats, groats and peanuts. Some of these items the average parrot completely disdained and they appeared to be added for the purpose of increasing the weight of the mix as it was sold by the pound. Other ingredients might have been suitable for farm fowl but were not ideal for exotic birds. As people learned more about feeding their parrots, they turned to more advanced pet shops, which permitted you to make up your own mixes from large bins containing a great variety of seeds and other items. In this way you could tailor the diet to suit your bird's own special tastes. Of course, just because a parrot liked Indian nuts didn't mean that they were particularly healthy for him.

Parrot owners became more knowledgeable about diet as articles and books on parrot nutrition appeared. Some veterinarians began to specialize in birds, and their advice also helped to improve birds' diets. The addition of fruits and vegetables to the daily food ration was a great improvement for parrots as most of these birds ate such items in the wild. Vitamin and mineral supplements designed for parrots (and not merely relabeled after being prepared for dogs or cats) also enhanced the life of our pets.

Offer your parrot a variety of nuts, seeds, fruits and vegetables. (Severe Macaw)

Fruits and Vegetables

As you might expect, parrots are fussy about which fruits and vegetables they will eat. Often the quality of the item has nothing to do with their diffidence in eating these healthy products. I usually put it down to the parrot's conservative nature and his unwillingness to make changes in his life. This is a good reason for starting fruits and vegetables early in the bird's life with you. In this way it becomes a normal activity and not something he has to learn later in life.

If possible, have an extra dish for fruits and vegetables so that they can be fed early in the day and removed at suppertime. This way, they do not remain in the cage for an inordinate length of time. The fruit and vegetable dish should also be washed daily as it will become sticky.

Fruits that have proven popular with many parrots include apples, peaches, grapes, cherries, strawberries, pears and firm-fleshed melons. In the case of apples, peaches and cherries it is vital that you remove the seeds or pits as they contain toxic substances.

Do not give your parrot especially large pieces of fruit. Rather, cut a small section and either place it in the parrot's dish or wedge it in a corner of the cage. If you have a protruding device (for example, something that holds a mirror or toy) you can impale the fruit chunk on it and in this way encourage the curious parrot to examine this newly arrived item. The first time I put an apple section in my African Grey's cage I heard him speaking to it before he bit into it.

I have purposely omitted suggesting any citrus fruits as many people believe that they cause loose stools. I am not positive if this is true, but with so many other excellent fruits available why take a chance?

Carrots are a crunchy, healthy treat for your parrot. (Congo Grey)

Vegetables such as green peas, corn, carrots, radishes, parsnips, beets, turnips and others can all be offered to parrots. Naturally, thorough washing is vital and they should also be cut into small sections. Smaller pieces are easy to handle and may also be more interesting to the parrot than one large piece of vegetable. It's a worthwhile idea to taste the fruits and vegetables that you provide for your birds to be sure they are fresh and wholesome. If you have any doubts about their freshness, dispose of them. If you are buying these products just for your birds, buy in small quantities; even the best storage container in a refrigerator vegetable or fruit bin cannot keep these products firm and desirable for any length of time.

If you get to your supermarket or vegetable store early in the day you may be lucky enough to find the owner or workers removing the tops of carrots, beets and radishes. Bring a plastic bag with you and ask if you can take them home. I specify early in the day as once they have been placed outside in the sun they will become useless for your purpose.

After bringing these highly nutritious and tasty greens home you can then repack them in small, sealable refrigerator bags. Keep these bags in your refrigerator's fruit or vegetable bin and each morning you can wash and rinse a bagful before offering them to the parrots. Remember to do the washing and rinsing just before feeding; if you wash the greens before you store them they will not last as long. I like to put these leafy greens on top of the bird's cage and let him pull them into the cage by himself to provide fun and nutrition at the same time. After you have had these greens for a while, check them more carefully before you feed. If in doubt, dispose of them as they cost you next to nothing in the first place.

If you decide to feed your parrot seeds, make sure they are fresh. (Gray-cheeked Parakeet)

Pellets or Seeds?

The use of pellets became popular in the mid-1980s, and eventually virtually every major parrot food packager offered a line of pelleted food along with their seed packages. Pellets are made by mixing appropriate nutrients with a binding agent and then passing the liquid mixture into an extrusion press, producing pellets of various shapes and sizes. Safe food coloring as well as enticing scents are also added, although these are probably more important to the parrot's owners than the bird itself.

Choosing between pellets and seed mixes is a personal decision. Some pellet enthusiasts note that the pellet provides a complete and balanced diet while seed proponents say that pellets deprive the parrot of the tactile pleasure of cracking seeds, which should be a natural part of his life. If a parrot has lived on seeds, it is sometimes difficult to get him to change over to pellets. I disagree strongly with those who suggest "starving the bird out" until he is forced to eat the pellets. A much more humane solution would be to offer a mix of pellets and seeds and get the best of both diets. When choosing a pellet diet read the label carefully. The protein content as well as the content of other nutrients varies according to the anticipated activity of the parrot who is to be fed. Thus, breeding parrots or young, very active parrots will be fed pellets with more protein than sedentary or older single parrots.

If you choose a seed diet be sure to note the contents of the mix and also choose a mix that is dated for freshness. Discuss the contents with a knowledgeable parrot enthusiast or your vet to be sure that you are feeding appropriately. If you are buying seed in bulk it will not be dated but you can ask for assurances from the shop owner and then test the seed at home by trying to sprout it

A SEED-CLEANING TIP

Don't assume that your parrot's seed cup is full just because it looks full. You may be leaving him with a food dish that has seeds on top and nothing but hulls beneath. If you wish to economize on seed you can purchase a seed cleaner. This is a simple device that uses the reverse air flow from a vacuum cleaner to draw air through a plastic box of waste seed collected over the week from your parrot's dish. The light hulls are drawn off while the edible seeds remain behind.

I prefer using the seed cleaner for a different purpose. Even the best seed will come with a certain amount of dust, dirt and debris that was picked up during harvest and packing. Using a seed cleaner will remove most of this matter. These devices can be found at your local pet shop or advertised in any bird magazine. You might even consider making one yourself, as the vacuum cleaner that supplies the air flow is the most complex part of the equipment.

(see sidebar). If less than 95 percent of a random handful fails to sprout, I would choose another source of seeds.

The Picky Eater

Not every parrot will eat each item you offer him. This can be very frustrating as you may have gone to great lengths to obtain fresh fruits or vegetables that wind up at the bottom of the cage without even a beak mark to show that they have been tasted. You may find that cutting an apple or a carrot into smaller pieces or different shapes and putting them in various areas of the cage will attract your curious bird. You should also keep trying, as our stubborn parrots are noted for ignoring a delicious item in October and going wild for it in March.

ELEMENTS OF A HEALTHY DIET

Seed mix

Pellets

Fresh vegetables

Fruits in smaller amounts

Vitamin supplements

Supplements

Even if you provide a pelleted diet or a perfect seed mix, both of which are presumed to have all of the vital nutrients, vitamins and minerals your parrot needs, you should still consider certain supplements. You have no guarantee that the parrot will eat a full ration of pellets on a daily basis or, in the case of a seed diet, that he will not skip over certain seeds.

VITAMINS

Vitamin supplements come in three common forms.

Powdered Vitamins These are dry and, if kept refrigerated in tightly closed containers, they will retain their viability at least until the expiration date shown on the bottle. Do not attempt to administer powdered vitamins by sprinkling them on seeds. If you do, most of the expensive powder will fall to the bottom of the seed cup and later be dumped out with the hulls and uneaten seeds. The best method for giving powdered vitamins is to sprinkle them on moist vegetables and fruits each morning. As a matter of good hygiene you will want to thoroughly wash any vegetables and fruits that you give to your parrot.

A good way to do this is to immerse them in a small container and then run a strong stream of warm water over them so that they tumble around to get all surfaces free of debris and any farm chemicals that may have been sprayed on them. Then place them on a few paper towels and, using a shaker container, sprinkle a light coating of vitamins on them. Do not choose vitamins that are designed for animals other than birds as vitamin requirements vary widely in the animal kingdom. Close the paper towel around the vegetables or fruits and as you bring them to your bird you can shake them a bit to ensure better distribution of the powder. Virtually all powdered vitamins have either a pleasant odor or no odor at all, so their presence should not put the parrot off his vegetables.

Adding supplements to your parrots' food will help keep them happy and healthy. (Hahns and Noble Macaws)

Oil-based Vitamins The oil-based vitamins have a strong cod liver oil flavor and odor, and both you and your bird may find this offensive. In addition I don't recommend using them during warm weather as the oil can become rancid. You can add oil-based vitamins to the water dish or use an eye dropper to cover the seeds or pellets in the bird's dish. The problem with doing this is that if the parrot objects to this vitamin mixture he will probably pass up both the water and his food.

Water-based Vitamins These have little or no odor and can usually be added to water or food without the risk of the parrot rejecting them. If you use his water dish and he is not a large consumer of water he may not take in much of the vitamin.

I would suggest sticking with a high-quality powdered vitamin designed for birds and use the moist vegetable and fruit technique. If, as suggested, you feed these items in the morning, you can make it a point to remove them when you feed the evening meal so that they do not lie around the cage for an inordinate length of time.

Parrots need calcium for a healthy beak and feathers. (Scarlet Macaws)

CALCIUM

Birds also require a reliable source of calcium. African Greys especially need extra calcium in their diets. This can either be provided by their normal food or ingested as a supplement. The skeleton of the cuttlefish (sometimes referred to as "cuttlebone") is very rich in calcium, as is ground oyster shell, which is sold for the same purpose. I am concerned about using either of these sources because of the danger that they came from waters polluted with toxins that cuttlefish and oysters filter through their bodies and then make part of their skeletons and shells. Consider instead a mineral supplement containing calcium and whose label clearly indicates that it is not produced from ground oyster shell.

WHEATGRASS AND SPIRULINA

Two supplements that have become popular in recent years are wheatgrass and spirulina. Spirulina is advertised as enhancing the presence of healthy bacteria in the digestive tract as well as providing many essential trace elements that may not normally be ingested by a captive parrot. Wheatgrass is a pleasant-smelling powder from the leaves of cereal grasses. It is rich in vitamins and minerals and is organically grown in mineral-rich soil.

SPROUTING

Sprouting is a simple task that both you and your parrot can benefit from. Visit a health food store and ask for small quantities of radish, sunflower, mung and other seeds. They can also sell you an appropriate sprouting jar as well as the mesh cloth needed to do the job. This simple equipment will come with full instructions for sprouting.

The technique involves soaking and washing the seeds and keeping them in a warm location so they will sprout. The washing is very important or the material will become foul. Sprouted seeds are not only tasty, they also have had their vitamin content increased. As noted above, seeds that do not germinate are not fresh and will provide a much lower level of nutritional benefit to your parrots.

When the seeds sprout (about 2–3 days), offer the sprouts to you parrot, and garnish your own sandwich with these nutritious tidbits.

Water

Water should be changed in the morning and in the evening. A good technique is to provide vegetables and fruit in the morning when you give your fresh water and remove the vegetables and fruits (which are perishable) at night when you replace the water from the morning and also supply seeds or pellets. Be sure to wash the water cups thoroughly, as they tend to build up an unclean film if you do not. You can check for cleanliness by rubbing your finger around the inside of the cup as you rinse out the detergent. If it has a slimy feel, wash and rinse it again. Of course, it is also absolutely vital that you completely rinse the cup free of any detergent or liquid soap that you use to clean with. If you are adding vitamins to the water it is even more important to change the contents of the water cup two or three times a day. In extremely warm weather I would suggest skipping the vitamins until the heat wave ends or switching to vitamins that can be sprinkled on food or moist vegetables for that period.

Treats

Special treats for parrots can help you to get a new bird who may be too timid or nervous to eat well started on a healthy diet. Consider raw corn on the cob (cut in one-inch wheels), peanuts (roasted are best to remove any possibility of mold), Indian nuts and taco chips, which parrots love because of their spicy taste.

If a parrot becomes ill and stops eating, ask your vet about a nutritional supplement paste. This is a sticky product that will adhere to the inside of the parrot's beak until he licks it away. In this way he is forced to take in some nutrients until the vet can bring him back to health.

Foods to Avoid

Of course, you must never give your parrot alcohol. Even in small amounts it can have a dangerous effect on such a small animal. Chocolate, too, can cause problems in small amounts. Avocados have been known to cause digestive problems in some birds. As I mentioned above, make sure to wash all fruits and vegetables thoroughly to remove any traces of pesticides.

Peanuts are a favorite parrot treat. (Severe Macaw)

chapter 6

Your Parrot's Physical Health

Hyacinth Macaw

Concerns about health for parrots and other birds differ from mammalian pets such as dogs and cats in a number of ways. Parrots have a high metabolic rate, and if they become ill you must act immediately to help them as their illness can progress rapidly with dire consequences if medical care is not provided.

To avoid tragedies it is wise to have a basic library of books on medical care for birds. (See our list of resources in chapter 9 for some recommended texts.) The purpose in having such books is not to help you avoid veterinary care if your bird becomes ill; rather, a well-written book on parrot or bird health care will enable you to recognize symptoms and conditions and to properly alert your veterinarian to what is happening to your bird. This sort of information can be invaluable to a veterinarian, because although his parrot patients can sometimes speak, they will not offer any useful information on what's bothering them.

Parrots can also confuse their owners about the state of their health by actually pretending to be healthier than they really are. This is a carryover from life in the wild, where an ill or weakened bird is often attacked by other members of the flock or outside predators. With that in mind, it is up to you to be aware of your bird's health.

Choose a veterinarian who has had extensive experience and education in avian medicine.

Avian Anatomy

A bird's body has many things in common with yours—you are both warm-blooded, and have basically similar sensory and internal organs. There are also many—obvious—differences between yours and your parrot's physical make-up. An understanding of your parrot's anatomy will enable you to better understand the physical stresses your bird is susceptible to, and the instructions and advice of your veterinarian. In addition, an

89

understanding of your bird's body and senses will give you insight into how your bird interacts with and perceives its environment.

YOUR PARROT'S SENSES

Sight

Birds' eyes are large compared to the size of their heads and they have very good eyesight; when flying, sight is the single most important sense. Birds can see some color, and can see details very clearly. Because parrots' eyes are located towards the sides of the head rather than in the middle, they tend to use one or the other. You'll notice your parrot tilting its head sideways to examine an object more closely.

Hearing

Birds do have ears. They are located behind and below the eyes. The feathers around the ears look slightly different and, if you part them, you will notice the ear openings. Birds' sense of hearing is well developed and they can distinguish different sounds much more rapidly than humans.

Taste and Smell

Smells dissipate quickly in the air, and a flying bird will have little opportunity to notice them. Because a bird is adapted for flight and life in trees, birds' senses of smell and taste (closely related to the sense of smell) are poorly developed.

Touch

Birds use touch frequently to interact with and explore their environments. Birds' beaks are useful for manipulating objects, and determining what is safe to play with, perch on or eat. Most parrots will also use their feet as we use our hands, to hold or feel out objects and textures.

FEATHERS

One of the reasons we are attracted to birds is because of their ability to fly. Feathers are a bird's specially adapted flight mechanism, an extremely effective evolutionary development.

A bird's feathers grow from specific follicles arranged in orderly rows (called *pterylae*). A bird has several different kinds of feathers which perform different functions of body covering and flight. Contour feathers cover the outside of the body, including the tail and wings. Contour feathers include flight feathers and body coverts, which cover the body and wings with a protective layer. Down feathers are the softer, fluffy feathers found on chicks and the undercoat of adult birds. They provide insulation. Semiplume feathers are the short, spiky feathers around the face and eyes.

Flight feathers are specialized contour feathers further divided into two groups. Primary flight feathers are the larger ones toward the outside of the wing. (These are the ones that need clipping.) Secondary flight feathers are closer to the bird's body, towards the inside of the wing, and give the bird control and support during flight.

Molting

Feather loss during molting is a normal happening. Molting does not mean bare spots and it generally occurs during the warmer months of summer. For pet birds, molting may be lighter and more irregular due to the constancy of light and temperature in their environments. During a molt, feathers are not lost all at once, but are lost and replaced in a pattern; in the wild, a bird with no feathers would be extremely vulnerable. The molting process should take about six weeks in all.

During molting, make sure the temperature is warm enough for your bird, who is without the insulation his feathers usually provide. He will probably preen more during this phase to encourage the new feathers to come out. During molting, your parrot may also require extra dietary supplements. Ask your veterinarian what he or she recommends.

MUSCULOSKELETAL SYSTEM

Your parrot's basic musculoskeletal structure is very similar to ours, but like much of the rest of the bird's anatomy, the musculoskeletal system contains many adaptations suited to flying. In birds, the bones that make up our arms have shifted and fused to become the wing bones. The breastbone, or sternum, is greatly enlarged to allow the attachment of the large pectoral muscles birds need for flying. Birds' bones are very light and some are hollow. This is an advantage during flight, but it also means the bones are very fragile and can be broken easily. Some bones actually contain air sacs; these are called pneumatic bones. They help to lighten the bird's body and to cool it.

DIGESTIVE SYSTEM

Birds have a very short digestive tract and high energy requirements. For these reasons, they need to eat often and a lot (relatively speaking, of course!).

Your parrot does not have teeth to help break up its food, but it uses its beak and tongue to crack and break up seeds and other plant matter. Your parrot's mouth lacks saliva to soften the food, so the food is moistened first in the esophagus where it travels next. From there, it is further broken down and moistened in the crop, which regulates the food flow to the stomach, providing a constant flow of digestible matter. The stomach has two parts: the proventriculus where digestive juices are added, and the gizzard, which breaks up the food into tiny pieces. In the small intestine the necessary nutrients are absorbed by the body. What's left over goes through the large intestine and into the cloaca, from where it is released through the vent.

Birds have only one opening for urine and fecal matter. This is why a bird's droppings are composed of both solid and liquid matter.

CARDIOVASCULAR SYSTEM

A parrot's heart is set up like a mammalian heart, with four chambers enabling efficient exchange of oxygen and carbon dioxide. However, a bird's heart beats much faster. A healthy large parrot's heart might beat up to 300 times a minute at rest!

RESPIRATORY SYSTEM

A bird's nostrils are located in the cere, the small cartilaginous oval above and behind the beak. The air enters here and then, once in the bird's throat, enters a small slit in the roof of the mouth called the choana, where it is warmed and filtered. Birds do not breathe like people do; the lungs do not expand and contract pulling air in and pushing it back out. Instead, the body wall expands and contracts pushing the air from the air sacs into the lungs and back out again, with a bellows-like motion. A bird must take two complete breaths to exchange the gases that humans and other mammals do in one.

Preventive Care

Good grooming and good preventive health care are necessary to help ensure your bird does not become ill. Taking proper care of your bird and doing your best to make sure it has a safe and healthy environment will go a long way toward making a happy, healthy parrot.

WING TRIMMING

Wing trimming is done to prevent flight. However, some birds still will attempt to flutter off a raised surface. For this reason and to increase the effectiveness of the procedure, it is preferable to trim both wings rather than only one. This way the bird is able to control its glide to the ground and land safely. Otherwise, your parrot may be prone to dangerous crash landings due to loss of balance and flight control.

Wing trimming must be done regularly in order to be effective, as new feathers grow in continually. All birds will have different rates of feather growth, but check every three or four months to determine if more trimming is necessary.

The proper method involves trimming the first five to eight primary flight feathers on each wing. The number of feathers clipped depends on the weight and size of the bird. The feathers that are cut are the long feathers towards the outside bottom of the wing, the primary flight feathers. They should be cut along the line indicated by the next layer of feathers above and over the primary flight feathers. These feathers are shorter and higher on the wing; they are called dorsal primary coverts.

Clipping is more difficult to do than it seems, and generally requires two competent people. If you have no experience clipping wings, have it done professionally. Watch the procedure carefully and learn how to do it.

BLOOD FEATHERS

When a new feather is ready to grow in, the first noticeable thing will be a projection of skin in the place where it will appear. Soon after, the feather will push through the skin. At first, this new feather is wrapped in a protective keratin sheath. It is called a blood feather, and each one contains its own artery and vein. *Never cut a blood feather.* When the feather matures, the blood supply dries up, and the outer sheath falls off. The feather is now a dead structure, like human hair or fingernails, and can be safely clipped.

NAIL TRIMMING

Birds' nails grow continually, just as humans' do, and will need clipping periodically. To check for overgrown toenails, place the bird on a flat surface. If the toenails are overgrown, the bird's toes will be elevated off the surface, as the curved toenail pushes them upwards.

You will need to assemble some supplies before you trim your parrot's toenails. Have a supply of styptic powder handy in case of bleeding, which results when the quick (the blood vessel running through the nail) is cut. The quick usually extends two-thirds to three-fourths of the way down the nail, and can be difficult to see if the nails are dark. If bleeding does occur, apply some styptic powder and watch to make sure the bleeding does not start again. You will also need some nail clippers: Human nail clippers work well for small birds, while dog nail clippers are recommended for larger birds.

Two people are required, one to restrain the bird and one to cut the nails. Trim just in front of the quick, if you can see it, and a little longer than three-quarters of the way down the nail if you can't. If you trim right in front of it and the nail is still too long, wait a couple weeks and trim close to the quick again. The quick will recede with each cutting.

BATHING

Bathing your parrot encourages preening, and most parrots enjoy bathing tremendously. As mentioned throughout, your parrot will probably love to be sprayed with a plant mister. If this doesn't seem to appeal, there are different methods you can try. A bowl filled with water placed by your parrot can provide suitable enticement. And of course, the bathroom is the perfect place. Birds may like the steaminess of the room while or right after you bathe, and many larger birds will even love to join you in the shower.

Bathe your parrot in the warmest part of the day, and never use soap or any other cleaning agent on your bird. These can destroy the natural oil coating on the feathers and result in dry, damaged plumage. Bird bathing solutions are available from bird product manufacturers; these aren't really necessary, however, and plain water is generally sufficient.

CHOOSING A VETERINARIAN

Don't wait for an emergency before selecting a veterinarian. As soon as you have decided to purchase a parrot you should make an effort to select a veterinarian who is skilled in treating birds. The ideal vet would be someone close to home who either treats birds as a subspecialty or who at least knows and likes parrots and has some background treating them. (I always smile at the term "avian vet," which has become so popular in recent years. It makes me envision Opus the Penguin dressed as a doctor.) Veterinarians who specialize in treating birds are individuals who have had appropriate courses in college and who have remained abreast of current avian health care information by participating in workshops and seminars and continuing their reading throughout their professional lifetime.

Have a travel crate on hand in case you need to transport your parrot to the vet. (Severe Macaw)

It is not always easy for a new bird owner to find an appropriately skilled veterinarian. I suggest you seek recommendations from friends and acquaintances who also own birds, or ask a local bird club for a reference. You may also contact the Association of Avian Veterinarians for information on a veterinarian who is closest to you (see chapter 9 for the address). Once you have made a list of several highly recommended veterinarians, you can ask them about their qualifications. A veterinarian who is confident of his skills should not take it amiss if you ask about his training and experience.

BE PREPARED FOR EMERGENCIES

Keep a travel cage or airline kennel available so that if you have to take your parrot to the vet you will have a suitable carrying container. Travel cages are temporary cages that set up and pack up quite easily. They are not designed to live in but are perfectly suitable for short-term use. Airline kennels look like dog carrying cases but have their wire portion sized for birds. These also work well, but I prefer the traveling cage as it is more comfortable for the parrot. Either one can be purchased at a pet shop or by mail from one of the many advertisers you will find in the various pet bird magazines.

Make Your Environment Safe for Your Parrot

In the case of a parrot, many problems can be avoided by thinking about danger in advance. Because your parrot will be spending much of his time in his cage, you can control a great deal of what he encounters. Be thoughtful about what you put into his cage, no matter if it's food, toys or treats. When your bird is let out of the cage to play and socialize, be sure he is in a safe environment without access to poisonous plants or other household dangers.

DANGEROUS TOYS

Make sure the toys you give your parrot to gnaw on and play with are safe and cannot be broken by strong beaks. Avoid chains with small links, as a parrot can catch a claw in these and either lose the claw or be left to suffer until you find him. Large linked chains pose no such danger. Leather thongs can also be useful but should always be thick enough so that they cannot be tied in a knot. If you can knot the thong the parrot can probably twist it into a noose with dire results.

Make sure the toys you give your bird cannot be broken apart into sharp pieces by a parrot's strong beak. (Red-front Macaw)

Flimsy toys with plastic or glass parts pose an obvious danger as parrots can chew and swallow the material. As a matter of good practice do not offer any toys with small removable parts.

97

SAFE FOOD

Do not feed anything that is not fresh. In the case of vegetables and fruit, don't offer you parrot anything that has wilted or gone soft. If you wouldn't eat it, don't offer it to your bird.

POISONOUS PLANTS

Be aware of your bird's normal behavior patterns. Changes in normal activity can mean illness, and you'll want to notice them right away.

Do not permit the parrot access to plants. Many houseplants are harmless, but there are also a great many that contain toxic chemicals. Make sure that your parrots avoid apricot and peach pits, as well as morning glory and four-o'clock seeds, which all contain a form of cyanide. Houseplants such as narcissus, hyacinths, daffodils and lilies are all poisonous, and the bulbs are extremely dangerous as they contain a high concentration of toxins. Castor beans, some cactus, mistletoe, wisteria and the berries and bark of the yew are also poisonous as are lilies of the valley and mountain laurel. There are actually so many potentially dangerous plants that a good rule is to keep your parrot away from any plant or plant product unless you personally know it is harmless.

If your bird has ingested one of these plants or any other toxic substance, call your veterinarian or Animal Poison Control Center (see the phone number in Chapter 9, "Resources") immediately. Some common signs of poisoning include staggering, convulsions, vomiting, diarrhea and coma.

AIR FILTERS

Parrots, like most birds, lose bits of feathers on a regular basis. During warmer months this loss is increased as they molt. Feather dust will be breathed in by both the birds and their owners and will also settle over objects in the bird room. It may even be moved throughout the house if there is a strong flow of air. Your parrot (and your family) may be sensitive to this dust and other bacteria in the house.

If you think this is the case, try an air filter. Various types are advertised in bird magazines. The better ones will remove pollen and household dust as well as bacteria and mold spores along with feather dust.

The Healthy Bird

Basic signs of a healthy parrot are being active and alert, and eating and drinking normally. If a parrot who has been doing all of the above starts to change this behavior, it should serve as a warning sign to you that all is not well.

ACTIVITY LEVEL

Parrots normally are quite active in the morning. Your healthy parrot will be doing acrobatics such as swinging, hanging upside down, and banging bells or other toys around in a violent manner. Chewing wooden toys and perches are all signs of feeling good, and a parrot in normal health will generally do all or some of these things. You know best what constitutes normal behavior for your parrot.

SELF-DEFENSE

Another sign of a healthy bird is self-defense. Even though your bird knows you well, he may swipe at you with his beak and squawk loudly if you attempt to reach in his cage and touch his foot or wing. Beware of changes in this type of behavior. A confident parrot who loses all aggressive tendencies is probably ill.

When I brought home Blondi, one of my Double-yellow Head Amazons, she was in a weakened physical condition and suffered from a number of minor health problems. She was a beautiful but passive bird who allowed me to hold her while I squirted vitamins and medication into her beak. Within three weeks, though she was still friendly, holding her was out of the question, and trying to force open her beak was a large error in judgment. Fortunately by this time she no longer needed medicating.

HOUSEHOLD DANGERS

Parrots need time out of their cage every day to stretch, explore and bond with you. Supervise your parrot while he is out of the cage, and make sure the environment you release him into is a safe one. It's best to take the following precautions:

Keep poisonous plants out of the room (including ivy, amaryllis, hyacinth, narcissus, and poinsettia). Safe plants include ferns and spider plants.

Keep electrical wires concealed.

Paint and furniture varnish are toxic, so don't let your bird gnaw on the furniture or painted objects.

Make sure all doors and windows are closed securely.

Make it a regular practice to carefully observe your parrot as you feed him and clean his cage. Has he become so docile that you can tweak his toe or flip his tail without him squawking a complaint? That's probably not a new level of tameness, but it could be a sign of illness if he never permitted these indulgences previously.

Signs of Illness
BEHAVIORAL CHANGES

Is he sneezing a lot? One or two sneezes mean nothing other than he is clearing his nostrils of dust. But if he sneezes repeatedly and if the sneezing produces mucus or fluid this is an obvious warning sign of a respiratory problem. Are his eyes as bright and busy as usual or are they half-closed and heavily lidded? Half-or fully-closed eyes at busy times of the day is a warning.

When a parrot is cold or sleepy he will fluff up his feathers to retain heat and, when really tired, turn his head and bury his beak in his feathers. A parrot who does this at the height of the day or evening, when he would normally be playing or eating, should be checked by your vet.

Most healthy parrots will take a nap at least once or twice during the day. At this time even a healthy parrot will often turn his head so that he can tuck his beak into shoulder feathers. Cockatoos usually fluff up the feathers around their cheeks when they are resting. These behaviors are typical and not signs of illness.

In the wild, birds and other animals will hide illness; if they reveal their weakness, they may be subject to attack from predators or even their own kind. Parrots in the home also hide indications of being unwell and will even play and react to you in an effort to keep up the subterfuge. If you know how the well parrot acts it will be easier to recognize the sometimes subtle changes in behavior that mean illness.

Physical Signs

In addition to the behavioral changes discussed above, look out for physical evidence of an illness or infec-

tion in your bird. Swelling around the nostrils, eyes or vent is not normal and may be the symptom of a respiratory infection. Weight loss and voice loss should be checked out by your vet immediately. Sudden loss of feathers that are not replaced is a situation in need of immediate attention. (See chapter 7 for more information on feather loss.)

A major change in the consistency of droppings is also an indicator of some-

A healthy cockatoo will ruff up his feathers around his neck when he is resting. (Moluccan Cockatoo)

thing wrong. After a few months you should be able to recognize what your bird's normal droppings look like. In general they will be part liquid and part semisolid, the central portion being the most solid. If the droppings suddenly become mostly liquid and remain that way, a problem may exist. Of course, if your bird has recently been eating a lot of fruit or other foods rich in water, the change in droppings may just be a result of diet. If in doubt cut off fruits, vegetables and vitamins for several days to see if there is a change. The rationale for stopping the vitamins is that they can, on occasion, also cause a change in the nature of the droppings, particularly when starting a new vitamin.

Emergency Management

You have chosen a competent vet and you've taken all the precautions to make your home a parrot-friendly one, but you must be prepared in the event of an emergency. Your bird's life depends on your quick, competent action. Make sure you are prepared with the proper materials and knowledge to take the best care of your parrot when it's needed most.

FIRST AID KIT

A well-stocked first aid kit is a necessity for any bird owner.

It should include:

a towel for restraint

styptic powder

cotton swabs

cotton balls

antiseptic wash

tweezers

eye dropper

syringe

scissors, sharp and pointed

"TOWELING" YOUR PARROT

Your parrot may need to be restrained if it is hurt or for more routine treatment, like toenail cutting or administering medication. Toweling is the best method of restraint, as catching your parrot with gloves can be very frightening for the bird.

Use an old towel draped over your hand. Approach the bird from behind and with a quick motion, grasp the bird around the head, with thumb and forefinger (under the towel) directly on the jawbone, palm on the bird's neck. This will immobilize the head and beak, thus preventing you from being bitten. Then adjust the rest of the towel firmly around the bird's body and wings, holding onto the rump and feet. *Never* grasp the bird around the abdomen or you may suffocate it. When you visit the vet for a check-up, ask him or her to show you how to perform this procedure.

EMERGENCY SITUATIONS AND FIRST AID

Bleeding

If, in spite of all your precautions, your parrot injures a claw, breaks a blood feather or cracks his beak, you will see bleeding. Since the drops of blood will splash from above to the bottom of the cage it will often look like more bleeding than is actually occurring.

A certain level of aggressiveness is normal for a healthy parrot. (Double-yellow Head Amazon)

Don't panic. Instead, get your first aid kit.

If the bleeding is because of a broken claw or broken feather that still has a blood supply (blood feather), try to staunch the flow using styptic powder on a wet cotton ball. This may work, but the parrot may resist because it stings.

If this is not successful, dip a cotton ball into the hydrogen peroxide and apply it to the area of the claw or broken feather where blood droplets appear to be forming. The peroxide will foam and help start coagulation almost immediately. In the case of a claw you can also dip the bleeding claw into a capful of peroxide with the same effect.

It is now important to keep the parrot as quiet as possible for as long as possible to allow full coagulation to take place. You can try putting out the light in his room so that he sits quietly and perhaps even goes to sleep. Before doing this put fresh, clean newspaper on the bottom of his cage so that you can later see at a glance if the bleeding has stopped. A bleeding beak, which is uncommon, should be treated in the same way. If you have caused the bleeding by cutting his nails too short, learn from the experience and cut less in the future.

Broken Bone

If your bird has one leg drawn up, or if his wing is drooping, suspect a broken bone. Take your bird to the vet to have the bone set. After treatment, move the perches to the bottom of the cage and restrict movement.

Diarrhea

If you notice your bird's droppings are more fluid

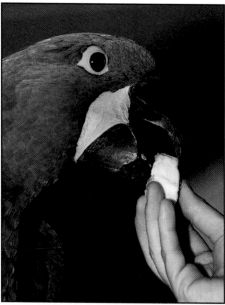

Unusually loose droppings can be caused by increased fruit in the diet, but if they persist, call your veterinarian. (Hyacinth Macaw)

than usual, determine if he ate something unusual that might have more water in it than he's used to. If his diet does not appear to be the cause, and the diarrhea continues, call your vet. Also, call the vet immediately is you notice blood in the diarrhea. Make sure you provide plenty of water to prevent dehydration.

Vomiting

If your parrot is vomiting, you will notice the sticky, semidigested food around your bird's beak and neck. If you notice any other symptoms, such as appetite loss or lethargy, or if your bird vomits repeatedly, call your vet immediately. Hold off on his food for a while and make sure he has plenty of water.

Shock

This may occur after the bird has been injured or traumatized. Signs of shock include rapid, shallow breathing, passivity and partly closed eyes. Call your veterinarian immediately. Avoid handling the bird as much as possible, as this may aggravate the condition and cause the bird to die.

Caring for the Ill Parrot

After your bird has received appropriate treatment from your vet, you can further help the healing process by providing good nursing at home. Your vet will provide you with instructions specific to your bird and its condition, but the following are general guidelines to keep in mind when caring for a sick bird.

KEEP YOUR PARROT WARM

First, make sure the healing bird's cage is not exposed to drafts, or cool air from other sources. Options you will want to consider with your vet include placing a heating pad around the bottom of the cage, draping the cage of larger birds with an electric blanket or setting up a heating lamp a few feet away from the cage.

ENSURE A STRESS FREE ENVIRONMENT

Keep handling to a minimum, and avoid unnecessary contact with the bird. Keep the cage in a quiet place, away from household noise and keep the light low enough so that the bird can rest as much as it needs to.

MEDICATING YOUR PARROT

As with any other medical procedure regarding your parrot, your veterinarian will show you how to administer medication. It is often useful, in addition, to have a written reference on hand to refresh your memory and confidence before you attempt the procedure.

Liquid Medication

First, restrain your bird using the toweling method described on page 102. Apply slight pressure where the upper and lower beak join to encourage the bird to open its mouth. Have the required amount of medication in a needleless plastic syringe, and insert it into the bird's mouth, over the tongue and to one side. Do not squirt it directly down the bird's throat as this may cause it to go directly into his lungs.

Special diets that are made with certain antibiotics can be very effective. However, burying the medication in the bird's food may be less effective because it is difficult to make sure the bird is consuming all the medication.

Another way to administer oral medication is to mix it in the bird's water, but this is not considered to be very effective. Sick birds may not drink as much water as usual, and you have no way of telling what amount of the medication the bird is actually ingesting.

Topical Medication
In this case, simply apply the medication to the affected area. Topical medication may be used for treating eye infections, sinus or skin problems.

Injection
This is the most effective way of administering medication to your parrot, but it may also be the most stressful, particularly for the owner. Many novice owners understandably feel unsure about injecting their birds, and should ask the veterinarian to demonstrate the procedure explicitly. However, with confidence, you will see that this method is actually quite simple.

Intramuscular injection is the most common way owners will be asked to inject their bird. Restrain your parrot, and lay it on your lap, chest up. Insert the syringe at 45 degree angle into the chest, and depress the contents into the muscle.

The Loss of a Parrot
Sooner or later, all parrot owners will have to face the pain that occurs when a beloved pet dies. Fortunately,

most bird owners never have to make the decision about euthanasia, as an ill or injured bird will often die very quickly. If this situation does arise, consult with your veterinarian to determine the most humane course of action for your pet.

Everyone will cope with his or her grief in a particular way. It often helps to talk with other people, especially other parrot owners. These people will understand the importance of the parrot in your life, and will appreciate the fond recollections of the times you and your bird shared.

Should you get another bird? Absolutely, but wait until you are ready to bring a totally new animal into your life. This is a new friend, not a replacement for the one you have lost. Let it be another opportunity to establish a close and rewarding relationship with the most magnificent of birds, the parrot.

chapter 7

Your Parrot's Mental Health

Blue and Gold Macaw

To paraphrase the famous psychiatrist who is my namesake, we might ask: "What do parrots want?" The answer is simple. A parrot wants the security of a life that does not change radically, and he also wants attention and the ability to interact with the individual or individuals who he perceives as family. If a baby parrot is hand-fed by you for even part of his weaning period he will in all likelihood consider you his parent. A good parent doesn't neglect his offspring, and if you do, your parrot will certainly resent you.

Many parrots want and enjoy physical closeness with their owners. This can amount to as little as the parrot having his neck scratched or it can extend to being held, cuddled, kissed and played with. Your parrot and you may develop routines and games that he will expect to followed each evening. If necessary, keep them short but try not to disappoint him.

There is nothing sadder than an unhappy parrot who is constantly in his cage and whose only relationship with his owner is having food and water replaced. That sounds like a prisoner in a cell, and actually is not a much better life. In addition to providing food and shelter for your parrot, you must also provide him with affection and stimulation. That's part of the responsibility of owning any pet.

The young bird you bring home from the pet shop or breeder will have learned many things in the few months that he has been alive. Hopefully all of them are good things. If not, it is possible to change bad habits or behavior in a humane and nurturing fashion.

Your Parrot Is Still Wild

Though your parrot may have been hand-fed, he is the offspring of parrots recently imported to this country from jungles abroad. He has thousands of years of wild heritage in his genes, and only a generation or two of domestication. While you are interacting with your bird, keep in mind that, though tame, he is basically a wild animal and will respond to much of his environment this way.

Easy Does It

This means that certain things may frighten or appear threatening to him. The most basic rule to remember is that you should always move slowly and avoid rapid, jerky gestures. If you are in a hurry, force yourself to slow down. The parrot has no idea of your need to save time, and banging dishes or slamming cage doors will only upset him.

Avoid moving your hand from above to touch the parrot. He has excellent eyesight but a hand arriving from above him may frighten him. In nature, enemies swoop down from above when attacking and your parrot will instinctively be afraid. It is much better if you let him see your hand arriving at the level of his feet. Once there and within his field of vision, you can slowly move your hand to his neck or belly without appearing dangerous.

Avoid activities that are frightening or unnatural to the parrot. Climbing, hanging from your finger, acrobatic

tricks and other engaging forms of behavior are all natural to him and he will perform and enjoy them. Forcing him to ride on a roller skate or little bicycle are activities that certain highly trained show birds perform, but they may not be ideal or enjoyable activities for your bird.

BE SENSITIVE TO HIS MOODS

Learn to read your parrot's moods. If he is tired or appears disinterested in play or training do not force yourself on him. He will not only fail to enjoy activity at a time like that but may be tempted to bite you if you persist. If you have noticed that a particular time of day is best for playtime or teaching, try to stick to that time.

Your parrot will enjoy performing tricks that come naturally to him, like climbing, swinging and hanging. (Hyacinth Macaw)

Feather Plucking

Feather loss in a particular part of the body may mean that the parrot is plucking his feathers or, if he lives with another bird, that he is being plucked by his cage mate. Self-mutilation is almost always caused by boredom or frustration. It is a very bad habit that is extremely hard to break. It is much better to prevent plucking by keeping your bird occupied and happy. If a parrot who has never plucked suddenly begins this type of behavior, try to think about any changes you have made in his life: cage location, degree of attention or entry into the family of a new parrot or even a new child. Once a parrot begins to pluck his feathers, the skin will become irritated which can lead to continued plucking even after the original cause is removed. In cases like this, frequent spraying of the bird with a plant mister filled with tepid water will help ease the irritation and stimulate new feather growth.

There are collars available that you can put on your parrot to prevent him from plucking his feathers. They are somewhat cruel, however, as they are very uncomfortable. Chances are the parrot will begin plucking again once the collar is removed.

Parrots enjoy spending time out of the cage with their owners. (Hahns Macaw)

Out-of-Cage Time

One aspect of keeping your bird content is to provide lots of opportunities for him to be outside of his cage. One way to achieve this is to open the cage door when you are cleaning the cage and doing the feeding chores for the morning or evening. The bird will almost always climb to the top of the cage to play. If you want to make life even more interesting you can obtain a "T"-stand perch. If you are more ambitious, try attaching a large swing to the ceiling of the bird room by using expansion bolts, which work well even with a plasterboard ceiling. Being out of the cage offers a change of pace, affords new views of life and provides the bird opportunities for more vigorous exercise than even the largest of cages will permit.

If their wings are not clipped, some parrots may even try to fly from the top of their cage to another location in the bird room. This is a great form of exercise but, unless done with care, can result in accidents and injuries. I would only recommend this for smaller birds such as Amazons and conures, as even a few flaps of the large wings of cockatoos and macaws will carry them a great distance and bring them up to a wall or window very quickly.

When the parrot is out of the cage be sure that he is not startled either by you or by other members of the family. If he is disconcerted, he may fly from wherever he is perched and hit a wall

Out-of-cage time provides an opportunity for your parrot to socialize, exercise and explore. (Severe Macaw)

or window. Even when you are working around the room, keep your eye on the parrot and what he is doing. Chewing paint, books, electric wires and furniture are all dangerous.

Most parrots will be quite willing to go back into their cages when you have put the fresh water and new food and treats in for them. To convince the recalcitrant parrot to return you can always hold out a recognizable goody such as a peanut or Indian nut. Just make sure that you stay alert, as some parrots may emulate my cockatoo, who often will go back in her cage, grab the treat and then rush out to the top a second time.

Teaching Your Parrot to Talk

Teaching a parrot to talk will always be limited by the basic speech capacity of the bird. This is a matter of genetics and age. If your parrot is young and belongs to a species that is talented, you will probably be highly successful in teaching him to speak. On the other hand, some parrots lack this skill and no matter how hard you work, the results will be limited.

Like most intelligent creatures, parrots learn by repetition. The ideal way for a parrot to learn to speak is for him to repeat the things you normally say to him each day. "Good morning," "Hi, bird," "Suppertime" and "No biting!" are all things a parrot will hear constantly. Pet shop parrots often greet people by saying "What's your name?" This is not because they are curious about a visitor's identity but because it's probably the sort of inane question that is asked of them many times a day.

If you speak a foreign language you may want to repeat certain words or phrases to the parrot in the language of your choice. Visitors will be amazed at this "foreign" parrot and the skill with which he speaks a language not native to them.

If you are anxious to increase your parrot's vocabulary and you do not particularly care whether what he says makes sense, you can use a tape recorder or similar device. Electronic supply stores sell continuous tape loops in various format lengths. These tapes will play over and over again without stopping. Obtain a six-minute loop and, for the sake of your sanity and the bird's well-being, record only about a minute of it with words and phrases you wish your parrot to learn. One- and two-syllable words and short phrases are easiest to learn. If you try for something too complex the bird may only repeat part of it and wind up saying cute but abridged words and phrases such as "want a cook!"

By recording only one minute of the six-minute tape you provide a rest period of five minutes between words and phrases. This is very important; if they are repeated without respite the parrot will eventually tune them out and learn nothing.

DR. IRENE PEPPERBERG AND ALEX

Dr. Irene Pepperberg is a researcher at the University of Arizona. Since 1977 she has been working with and training an African grey parrot named Alex. Her achievements with Alex have been extraordinary. He can currently identify shapes and colors, and distinguish quantities up to six. He can name about forty specific objects. He makes requests and rejects suggestions (with a resolute "No") of Dr. Pepperberg and her staff. Dr. Pepperberg's research demonstrates that parrots are certainly intelligent creatures, capable of sophisticated comprehension and communication.

Don't expect your bird to learn everything on the tape. After about a week record over what you originally had and give him some new things to learn. Because parrots are notorious for failing to speak when visitors are in the room, try listening outside his doorway and you may be delighted to hear him saying clever things he never says in your presence.

A word of caution: Obscene words are generally short expletives that are easy for a parrot to learn. This type of speech is funny only in comic strips and should be avoided. It is far from humorous when children or other visitors come to admire the parrot.

DO THEY UNDERSTAND?

There have always been arguments about whether or not parrots understand what they are saying. In spite of the accomplishments of Alex (a well-publicized talking Grey who has learned to count and recognize shapes), it appears that these loquacious birds only appear to understand what they say as they are clever enough to repeat things at the right time and even in the correct sequence. Thus, many times their remarks will yield an eerie sense of legitimate conversation. A Grey who daily hears and knows that his mistress will answer the ring of the phone with "Hello" will probably do the same.

Special Considerations for the Re-homed Parrot

Buying a hand-fed baby parrot is not the only route to owning a fine pet bird. Even though importation has ceased, parrots sometimes do change families. Reasons for parting with a parrot might include the arrival of a new baby (and the resulting need for a quieter household); the discovery that the dander from a parrot's feathers is causing or exacerbating respiratory problems; the move from a private home to an apartment where noise cannot be tolerated; or even a change of lifestyle in which frequent travel precludes owning any pet. All are reasons why older birds sometimes appear on the market.

Another reason is that some individuals who purchase a tame baby bird lack the skills or will to work with the bird and keep it happy and tame. As a result, the bird, who wants nothing more than attention and an opportunity to play and interact, may become hyperactive and in his excitement may nip when the owner finally takes him out of his cage to play with him. A vicious cycle then ensues because nobody wants to play with a bird whose

behavior may vary from friendly to biting. The result is usually that the bird is sold or given away.

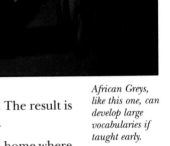

African Greys, like this one, can develop large vocabularies if taught early.

If the bird is fortunate he will wind up in a home where the new owners are sympathetic and understand that he has been traumatized. This probably sounds like a sad adoption story out of Little Orphan Annie, and to an extent it is similar. We're dealing with a creature who has the capacity for friendship and loyalty and a

115

desire for interaction. Is there hope for him? Absolutely!

The first thing to determine is the gender of the person who previously owned the parrot. I'm not quite sure how they do it but parrots seem to be able to differentiate between male and female humans as well as children and adults. If the older parrot you have purchased was frightened, mistreated or poorly treated by a male he may do better with a new female owner. The reverse, of course, is also true.

When you let your parrot out of the cage, make sure the room he's in has been parrot-proofed. (Severe Macaw)

When you first attempt to introduce yourself to and work with the mature parrot be sure to avoid wearing items that may frighten him. Long dangling earrings, dark sunglasses, a reversed baseball cap—all these

should be kept out of the bird room. Parrots are the most conservative animals on earth. If you appear bizarre to them they will in all likelihood avoid contact with you.

After you have brought this new, older bird home, bring him to the room where he is going to live and replenish his food and water dishes. Then give him a period of time to relax and look around the area. Don't overwhelm him with new toys in an effort to be attentive; these will be just something else to adjust to as he determines whether or not the toy will attack him.

After a few hours, one member of the family (ideally the one who will be feeding and spending the most time with him) should come back to the bird room and open the cage door. This move and all other activities should be done slowly and without sudden movements. Try sitting in a chair near the cage and watching him as he watches you. You might even bring a book you can read (or pretend to read) as you wait for him to consider coming out of his cage. Your main goal at this point is for the parrot to get used to you and to realize that you pose no threat and mean him no harm.

If the parrot comes out of the cage and moves to the top, which is the normal pattern of parrot behavior, stand close to him and note whether he moves away or stands his ground. If he moves away sit down and wait a bit longer. If he remains near you slowly bring your hand up to the level of his feet and try to touch his feet with the side of your hand. Three things are vital at this point: Move slowly, use the side of your hand so that you are not pointing a finger at him like a weapon and do not flinch if he brings his beak toward you. The parrot's beak is a climbing tool as well as a seed-cracking device, and if he lowers his beak toward your hand he may be getting ready to climb aboard; pulling away will set things back.

A re-homed bird will require patience and a gentle touch to adjust to his new home. (Gray-cheeked Parakeet)

Let us assume that the tender scene described above does not take place. The parrot does not come out of the cage and does not show any interest in you. After spending a reasonable amount of time sitting in the room, move to the next step. Close the door of the room you are in, carefully lift the cage off whatever surface it is on and move it to the floor. Then return to your chair and repeat the earlier procedure of patient and quiet waiting. At some point the bird will again climb out of the cage. This time, sit on the floor next to him. Next, close the door to the cage so he cannot retreat back in and slowly place your hand behind him in an effort to more or less gently urge him from the top of the cage down to the floor. No actual physical contact is necessary as he will move away from your hand while uttering complaints.

Once he is on the floor with you it is very likely that he will climb on your leg, arm or hand if you offer these substitute perches. When successful contact is made you can either return him to his cage for a break or continue your efforts to show him just how nice it is to be with this new two-legged creature who obviously likes him. A food treat such as a peanut, taco chip or Indian nut would also be appropriate at this time.

TRAINING TIPS

Make sure your training environment is safe and secure

Start off with simple tasks

Keep training sessions short and upbeat

Teach tasks that your bird can perform naturally

Offer lots of praise and—less frequently—food rewards

Keep these acclimation sessions fairly short as in the beginning they will be a strain on both you and the parrot. Fifteen or twenty minutes of activity are more than sufficient, but the time can be extended as you and the parrot progress in your work. If you remember to avoid jarring or frightening approaches, all the time spent with your parrot should move the relationship forward. It may take weeks, but each sign of calm trust will make it all worthwhile. When he shows his acceptance of you on a regular basis, you and your parrot can continue to enhance the relationship by kind and thoughtful behavior on your part as you go through the normal daily activities of feeding, cleaning and playing.

Some parrots are labeled "broncos," an allusion to the wild horses of the American West that are difficult for cowboys to tame (break). Parrot broncos are not just born; they are made by errors in judgment or bad treatment. Thinking in terms of breaking them can only make matters worse.

Most people should not purchase a "bronco" as it is not always possible for these birds to become pets. You cannot believe the shopkeeper who tells you that a bird's wild and frightened behavior is just shyness that will improve or disappear when he is taken into your home. If you have great confidence in your skills and patience and the price is low, it may be worth a try, but make sure that you get a money-back guarantee from the owner of the pet shop.

Beyond

the
Basics

chapter 8

Recommended Reading

Books

Books, no matter what the topic, can always be a great source of information. Some informative books that you can get through your public library or request through any major bookstore include:

Alderton, David. *A Birdkeeper's Guide to Parrots and Macaws.* Morris Plains, NJ: Tetra Press, 1989.

Doane, Bonnie. *My Parrot My Friend: An Owner's Guide to Parrot Behavior.* New York: Howell Book House, 1994.

Doane, Bonnie. *The Parrot in Health and Illness.* New York: Howell Book House, 1991.

Freud, Arthur. *All About the Parrots.* New York: Howell Book House, 1980.

Freud, Arthur. *The Complete Parrot.* New York: Howell Book House, 1995.

Gallerstein, Gary A., D.V.M. *The Complete Bird Owner's Handbook.* New York: Howell Book House, 1994.

Lantermann, W. and S. *Cockatoos, A Complete Pet Owner's Manual.* New York: Barron's, 1989.

Magazines

Monthly and bimonthly magazines such as *Bird Talk* and *Bird Breeder* are published by Fancy Publications, 3 Burroughs Ave., Irvine, CA 92718, (714) 855-8822. Write or phone them regarding subscriptions or pick up a copy of either magazine at your newsstand. The information in these publications is current and the advertising will lead you to many products that will be valuable to you and your parrot. Another bonus is the large number of classified ads in each of these magazines. Many of them offer parrots at excellent prices. Caution is the watchword here, and I recommend that you buy from a breeder close to home so that you can visit and see the parrot you are purchasing before you part with your money.

These magazines also publish information on the many bird shows that take place each year throughout the United States and Canada. Some are small shows with fewer than one hundred exhibitors, while others are major exhibitions with thousands of birds and exhibitors in attendance. Shows are great places to learn, exchange information, see other people's birds and find out about bird clubs in your own area that you might wish to join. Most shows take place in October and November, as that's when exotic birds look their best. Go through the list of shows and make plans for an exciting and informative show season.

chapter 9

Resources

Veterinary Information

If you cannot locate a veterinarian who treats birds, contact the Association of Avian Veterinarians at PO Box 811720, Boca Raton, FL 33481; phone (407) 393-8901, and ask for a recommendation.

Bird Clubs

There are hundreds of bird clubs meeting on a regular basis. Some are specialty clubs such as the African Lovebird Society or the Long Island Parrot Society. Others are all inclusive national clubs, such as the National Cage-Bird Show, Inc., which moves its annual exhibition to different regions each year. Check *Bird Talk* for the addresses as well as the phone numbers of contact people for these clubs. You will find that they will give you a gracious welcome.

African Lovebird Society
P.O. Box 142
San Marcos, CA 92079-0142

African Parrot Society
P.O. Box 204
Clarinda, IA 51632-2731

Amazona Society
P.O. Box 73547
Puysllup, WA 78376-4016

American Federation of Aviculture
Dept. BT
Box 56218
Phoenix, AZ 85079-6218

Asiatic Parrot Society of America
734 Boulder Hwy., Ste. 400
Henderson, NV 89015

Bird Clubs of America
P.O. Box 2005
Yorktown, VA 23692

Cockatoo Society
26961 N. Broadway
Escondido, CA 92026

Eclectus Society
215 Lilac Dr.
El Cajon, CA 92021

National Cage Bird Show Club, Inc.
25 Janss Rd.
Thousand Oaks, CA 91360

National Parrot Association
8 N. Hoffman Lane
Hauppage, NY 11788

The Real Macaw Parrot Club
(201) 265-1392

Avian Information Management (AIM)
Dept. BT
P.O. Box 369
Felton, CA 95018-0359
(800) 246-5577

Avian Information Management can help you find a bird club in your area.

Parrot Conservation Organizations

United States World Parrot Trust
P.O. Box 341141
Memphis, TN 38184

Other Organizations

Association of Avian Veterinarians
P.O. Box 811720
Boca Raton, FL 33481

Write to the AAV for a recommendation of an avian veterinarian in your area.

Parrot Rehabilitation Society
P.O. Box 620213
San Diego, CA 92612-0213

The Parrot Rehabilitation Society rescues and rehabilitates abused and neglected parrots.

National Animal Poison Control Center hotline
(800) 548-2423

You are well prepared for just about anything at this point. Go out and find that parrot that you've always wanted to own, buy him, bring him home to a well-prepared cage and plan to enjoy each other's company for many years.